BECOMING WHO YOU ALREADY ARE...

YOUR HOLY IDENTITY

BECOMING WHO YOU ALREADY ARE...
YOUR HOLY IDENTITY

Reverend Juliana Taylor, Ph.D.

Copyrighted Material
Becoming Who You Already Are... Your Holy Identity
Copyright © 2019 Reverend Juliana Taylor, Ph.D.
All Rights Reserved.

No part of this publication may be reproduced, stored in a retrieval system or transmitted in any form or by any means—electronic, mechanical, photocopying, recording, or otherwise—without prior written permission from the publisher, except for the inclusion of brief quotations in a review.

Enforcing Grace Ministries
Enforcinggrace.com
Los Angelos Ca.,USA

ISBN 978-0-578-53722-1 (paperback)
978-1-7923-3793-2 (ebook)

Printed in the United States of America

Acknowledgements

This book would not have been possible without the courageous people that have been willing to step out into a new realm of faith and adventure with God. These unique spirit-led beings chose to have a resurrection experience with their own Christos, the Christ within their Holy Identity. They brought joy, revelation, and more faith into my life with each and every step of faith that they allowed me to encounter with them.

From Jane triumphing over her food allergies to Leslie overcoming her bronchitis in an instantaneous healing, to Tommy transforming from being an alcoholic to a light bearer, I am grateful for their intelligence and dedication. I will never forget any of them.

I still speak weekly with Kathleen and she continues to expand her spiritual horizons in both her marriage and in her personal acquisition of dominion on Earth. I acknowledge her walk with God and her contributions to this material.

In my heart, Charlotte's story is the most revealing of all our desires, as she shared the deep longings of her heart. As she confronted her fear of aggression, I watched her be restored and sanctified from her past and her severe childhood traumas. Appropriating her own faith and willingness, she became the loving vessel and woman of God that she was predestined to be.

I must mention Mike and his brave subjugation of medical beliefs in his battle with a badly wounded knee.

There was the wild victory of Lily, confronting her demons, or what she believed to be demonic attacks, with a primal warfare, one contrived by the Master Himself.

Then there is Jacob, who loved animals and almost lost his precious cat Pita, but his faithful heart and new understanding of God's laws of righteousness rescued them both!

Had these precious folks, and other wonderful vessels, not risen in their Holy Identity and allowed their spirits to be led by God, to rule, reign, and conquer their inner oppositions, there would be no story to tell!

If there were no transformations, healings, or renovations of heart, mind body and soul, there would be no demonstrations of my prophetic premise of Holy Identity.

Without demonstration there is no fruit, no reality.

However, these humble and consecrated souls have truly served and esteemed God in a unique and new way. They have contributed to bringing to Earth a new path of healing, a new way to receive our divine rights, a way of the spirit to live in grace and authority in the now, to be who we truly are: The righteousness of God in Christ.

I am eternally grateful for their violent faith. I am honored at having been considered by God, to fellowship and facilitate in their purposes, healings, and heartfelt connections.

*I dedicate this book to the one who
beckoned me to write it.
To the one that spoke these words into my heart
and mind every day for six years.
To the lover of my soul, restorer of my life,
and the one that I joyfully serve.
The Lord of all, Christ Jesus.*

Preface

This book is about you! Who you truly are, who you were created to be, who you always were, and, most importantly, who you are not. It is about your power, authority, healing, spiritual fruits, and the ultimate reclamation of your divine rights.

Becoming who you already are, Your Holy Identity, is about your spirit accomplishing what it came here to do: win the battle that you came to win, the war between the flesh and the spirit.

> *"For the flesh desires what is contrary to the Spirit,*
> *and the Spirit what is contrary to the flesh.*
> *They are in conflict with each other, so that*
> *you are not to do whatever you want."*
> —Gal. 5:17

God is about to expand your heart and raise your consciousness to His, so that you may become your innate spirit being, the person you were created to be, in the fullness of your Holy Identity, the new creature in Christ.

> *"Therefore if any man be in Christ,*
> *he is a new creature: old things are passed away;*
> *behold, all things are become new...."*
> —2 Cor. 5:17

This is an instruction manual to assist you in learning to identify your real enemy and the lifelong battle you have always been fighting. You will learn to appropriate your God-given innate spiritual authority, to bring your opposition under subjection.

This material has the capacity, and intent, to renew your mind to your authentic spiritual self. It is a prophetic work of God's Word of "Holy Identity," a renovation for your unconscious mind. It is also a means of resurrecting your spirit, a reminder and edifier of your authority and divine rights in Christ. This Word of renewal is predestined to create a "Transformational and Radical Redemption," a higher ground, for those who are willing, ready, and fated to receive it.

You will begin to identify the carnal mind as a master of holding back any sincere move of God. You will now be able to go forward, to move ahead, as you gain power over your generationally inherited ego mind of fear and doubt—a serious spiritual power, the power of God!

I like to call this deliberate interference with our ability to access our divine connection "The Holding-Back Syndrome." The Bible calls it "enmity against God."

Preface

> *"Because the carnal mind is enmity against God:*
> *for it is not subject to the law of God,*
> *neither indeed can be."*
> —Rom. 8:7

The old nature, the Impostor of your identity, can only be conquered by faith, not by a confession of words, not by intellectual beliefs, and not by vain repetition of ritualistic prayers or seminars. We have been coddling, even embracing, the opposition, not identifying it, not calling it out. That is ending now with you! We, as the people of God, are obliged to put an end to this bowing down to the imprudence of deception. We will stop allowing the carnal ego mind to attempt to reestablish the law.

> *"Wherefore the law was our schoolmaster to bring us*
> *unto Christ, that we might be justified by faith."*
> —Gal. 3:24

We as spirit beings are innocent, fresh. We come to the Kingdom as a child of God, in wonderment and awe, excited to achieve a new purpose. This drives the old self, the old creature, the carnal mind, crazy. It loses control, and that is exactly what is supposed to happen. We will increase in spirit, in Christ, and the flesh will decrease. This is called "dying to the flesh."

> *"He must increase, but I must decrease."*
> —John 3:30

We will now begin to move past generational victimization. The Impostor of our authentic identity is being exposed, so that we may conquer and overcome it, by taking our power back from it! Only then are we able to enter into a spiritually established new moment, a radical "Transformational Redemption."

Many people have become utterly disgusted with empty religious rhetoric, with repression, with faking it. They have become disgusted with their old nature keeping them from spiritual vibrancy.

Many have had to hit the religious rock bottom, an utter disconnection from the Christ within, a feeling of despair deep in the soul, a fear of having nothing spiritually tangible left...

We want to be radically alive and inspired by an encounter with God. Nothing else will satisfy us. This is our divine right and has already been imparted to our holy essence.

The world is calling out to God, for God to reinstate us! Here comes the clincher, here comes God's plan, for in the end, God gets what He wants... He's God!

Beloved brothers and sisters, this new move is going to happen the way it always has, the same way God has always saved man, His Earth, and changed the world over and over again through faith and righteousness.

This time, it will be through you, through violent faith, in divine time, in a spiritual action that moves ahead, one that has the power to conquer all that opposes you. This is the power of a living God, Immanuel, the Christos in you, will partner with you to claim your authority over all that would hold you back from your divine rights. You are going to learn how you can cut to the chase of regeneration power and evoke a healing miracle.

You are going to take your power back, from the generational old creature, by your personal move ahead, a moving ahead with your violent faith in a Divine Retaliation!

> *"He hath made every [thing] beautiful in his time:*
> *also he hath set the world in their heart,*
> *so that no man can find out the work that*
> *God maketh from the beginning to the end."*
> —Ecclesiaste 3:11

Contents

Acknowledgements v
Preface ix

Section I   *Your Holy Identity* 1
      1. Becoming Who You Already Are 3
      2. Your Divine Rights 9
      3. Dogma and Guilt. 15
      4. The Impostor and Religious Christianity 25
      5. The Master of Your Temple 35
      6. Enforcing Your Spiritual Identity 43
      7. Your Common Denominator Is Love 49
      8. You Are Not Your Body. 67
      9. Identify Who You Truly Are 75
     10. Who You Are Is Not Broken…Don't Fix It. 83

Section II   *Righteousness Consciousness* 89
     11. Identifying Sin Consciousness 91
     12. You Do the Talking 95
     13. Familiar Spirits of Fear 107
     14. The Trigger Is the Bow 113
     15. Righteousness Consciousness versus
          Sin Consciousness 121
     16. There Is Therefore Now. 137
     17. Christos-Sanity 161

	18.	Laying the Idols Down 169
	19.	Righteousness Consciousness and Repressed Love . 181
	20.	Holy Identity Stand ("HIS"). 191

Section III	*(Part I) Divine retaliation* 197	
	21.	The Healing Power of Divine Retaliation 199
	22.	Violent Faith 201
	23.	The Cross of Love 205
	24.	Conquering Doubt. 207
	25.	Decomposing Trauma 213
	26.	Restoration via Retaliation 219
	27.	Confronting with Your Christos 223
	28.	Laying the Idols Down 229
	29.	A Powerful Weapon 233
	30.	The Holding-Back Syndrome. 235
	31.	High in the Christos 237
	32.	The Redirection 241
	33.	Dominion on Earth. 245

Section III	*(Part II) Victorious Tales of Divine retaliation* 247	
	34.	Jane's Story of Conquering Food Allergies 249
	35.	Lily's Story of Confronting Demons. 263
	36.	Tommy's Story 269
	37.	Leslie's Story 279
	38.	Jacob's Story 285
	39.	Charlene's Story 293
	40.	Kathleen's Story 301
	41.	Mike's Story 307
	42.	Authentic Surrender 315
	43.	About the Author. 319

Section I

YOUR HOLY IDENTITY

Chapter 1

Becoming Who You Already Are

Becoming who you already are may be as simple as identifying who you are not. You are who you are, and you cannot possibly be anyone else. Whether you are enlightened to this fact or not, you are a spirit.

You are your spiritual and Holy Identity. You are a spirit person, a radically alive, radiant, and loving being. You are a spirit being with all power over deceptions and all power over illnesses and fears. You are a complete and whole spirit being with authority over your mind, your emotions, your body, and your entire past. That is your absolute truth!

You have a choice and a divine assignment to arrest the voice of all that would claim that you are not a spirit being. You can choose to identify all that would unjustly infer that you are not your innate spiritual essence and authority. Who you are in your Holy Identity is more than able to hear, deny, and stop agreeing with any thoughts or words that would have you reduced to a mere mortal, powerless soul, which you are not.

Inner Opposition

Who would want to undermine your God-given spiritual identity? Who would want to oppose it? There is an inner Impostor, a counterfeit of your identity, pretending to be you. There is an Impostor of your spirit who is battling you for your divine position of righteousness, for your God-given grace. The Impostor of your spirit is attempting to subvert your true identity.

You are not your body. You are a spirit, having a spiritual experience in a body. Your physical form does not define you. Your spirit is eternal, immortal and separate from the limitations of gender, appearance, color, descent, nationality, generationally inherited DNA, sexual orientation and medical diagnosis. Your true identity is not of the flesh but of the spirit.

> *"The first man was made a living soul;*
> *the last Adam a quickening spirit."*
> —1 Cor.15:45

That is you, my fellow humans. You are a quickened spirit! The Impostor pretends to be you by always attempting to convince you that it is you. That is its power, a sophisticated, premeditated con job. It is always opposing your spirit and striving to create unholy mesmerizations in your mind. If the Impostor has succeeded to beguile you up until now, you might be living the life of your ancestors, by repeating their errors and past failures, and parroting their words and behaviors. This is not your purpose. This is not even your true existence.

Sometimes, the Impostor is referred to as your ego mind, the fear mind, the generational mind, the old self, the flesh-carnal mind, the old creature, the mortal mind, or even the Devil. The Impostor is all that opposes your spiritual identity. In the Bible, it is referred to as "enmity" against God, the carnal mind of mortal man; it is man disconnected from spirit. Do not allow semantics to distract you from your empowerment. If thoughts attempt to distract you from identifying or naming the Impostor, that is just the Impostor itself. It is always trying to distract you from separating yourself from who you are not. You are not this counterfeit. Perhaps it is attempting to distract you right now. If it is, just notice and acknowledge the attempt. Do not give it place. Instead, come back and continue to identify who you are not.

A Spiritual Awakening

As this enlightened truth of your authentic identity is being imparted, the Impostor's seduction of error is beginning to end. A spiritual awakening, a coming out of denial of your true self, is being created. It is an awareness that you may have had in your dreams. It is a knowing in your heart. This awakening is an awareness that knows who you truly are, an awareness that compels you to choose to separate yourself from this "Counterfeit Consciousness," the Impostor of your spiritual being. This very awareness has the power to resurrect your oppressed spirit and to restore it. It has the power to restore "you" to your righteous position, to your proper God-given place above the carnal ego fear mind, above the mind of the Inner Impostor.

"For the flesh lusts against the Spirit, and the Spirit against the flesh: and these things are opposed one to the other, that ye should not do those things which ye desire."
—Gal. 5:17

Perfected

There is absolutely nothing wrong with you, except that you might be being seduced into believing that there is.

"You are the righteousness of God in Christ"
—Rom. 3:22

You are called with a holy calling. Everything you need you already have, for it is written in your heart. You are full of love. You are pure and holy. You have divine health. You have authority over everything on this Earth and, certainly, over your body, your thoughts, your mind, and your own well-being. You are here with a divine purpose and a vessel job description.

"Written not with ink but by the Spirit of the living God, not on tablets of stone but on tablets of flesh, that is, of the heart."
—2 Corinthians 3:2, 3

You are a chooser in every new moment of what you think and what you will allow yourself to receive. If words are being imparted to your heart that are undermining or disempowering, you need only to examine your own thoughts in your divine mind and choose not to receive any Impostor input. You do this by simply denying its oppressive words and making a watchful decision to think—to simply take over your thoughts. You can choose to deny or refute any undermining thought. You are the chooser of your thoughts and you have the power to change your consciousness at any given moment.

You Are the Christos!

The anointing of God abides in you. The power to be the spirit person that you actually are is within you. It does not come from any teachings or from another individual.

> *"The anointing that you received from Him abides in you, and you have no need that anyone should teach you. But just as the same anointing teaches you concerning all things and is true and is no lie, and just as it has taught you, you shall abide in Him."*
> —1 John 2:27

Recognize and Identify

Disagree vehemently with deception. Recognize and identify the fear-thinking addiction of the Impostor and the lying symptoms that it creates in your body and stop its lies. As you begin to make the connection between the Impostor's fear-thinking and its effects on your body, you will be able to arrest its mental attack and you will see pain, depression, and illness bow to you. You are about to embark on the most authentic and empowering journey of your life!

Chapter 2
Your Divine Rights

This book is about your divine rights that are already positioned in your spirit in your "Holy Identity." Your spiritual identity has within itself the full access to the grace of God and your God-given divine authority.

Your survival here on Earth, your prosperity, joy, love, and health, all depend on your ability to identify who you are. Who is talking? Who is hearing? Who is thinking? Who is planning your day? Who is planning your future? Who is leading, who you are and who you are not? You are the real thing.

You Are Not the Impostor

This is a God-given revelation that has the power to change your spiritual beingness. A counterfeit is not real. It is inauthentic; It is a fake. An Impostor is something that is trying to pretend to be something that it is not. In your spiritual situation, the Impostor wants to be you. It is not you. You are authentic. You are righteous. You are divine. You are in impeccable, emotional, and spiritual integrity.

> *"You are Incorruptible seed."*
> —1 Peter 2:3

Who you are can neither compromise nor sin; it is impossible!

> *"The spirit cannot sin!"*
> —1 John 3:9

This Impostor of your identity is nothing more than a false prophet of fear, worry, and doubt. It is a self-proclaimed ruler, an idol, of the carnal mind. The Impostor is an actor, a performer of material mesmerization. It is without authenticity or integrity. You are here now and predestined to be in this new moment; you have been called to expose this Impostor and to take your power back from it.

Taking Your Power Back

If I say take your power back from illness, take your power back from pain, take your power back from depression, take your power back from doubt, take your power back from allergies, fear, anxiety, addictions, migraines, arthritis, fatigue, religion, indecision, condemnation, guilt, the past, confusion, lupus, cancer, and even from heartbreak, it is all the same.

To take back your power from who you are not, the Impostor of your identity, is to take your power back from all that creates disharmony in your life. You will do this by identifying it and calling its bluff. What will be left standing (literally) is who you truly are.

The Impostor has an addiction to powerlessness, to giving power away, and to bowing. That is its innate nature, its mortal DNA. Don't take it personally—it is the human condition. Yet always be aware that you are an immortal spirit.

You Have and You Are the Love of God

You are pure love. You love everybody around you. There is not one person on this Earth for whom you don't have the love of God because you are the image and likeness of God in pure love. That is who you truly are. You cannot be anything else. There is nothing you can do to be anything else. You can only be deceived into relinquishing your authenticity, your integrity, and your identity to the inner Impostor of your Divine Consciousness for a moment in time—and then you can choose to take it back with your God-given authority.

The Warrior in You

This is where destiny meets the seasoned spiritual road of the warrior, your innate spirit being, you, and leads you to decide that this is the time to stop living as the old creature, controlled by "Sin Consciousness," guilt, condemnation, and victimization. These are the characteristics of the Impostor. This is the time for you to exorcise the erroneous influence of your inherited generational seed, a corruptible seed. You are not your parents' victimizations! You have been redeemed from the old creature and its inherited deceptions.

The Perfect Law of Liberty

This is your new moment where the flesh bows to you, the spirit person: "the new creation," which is in "The Perfect Law of Liberty." This is called "Righteousness Consciousness," partaking freely of the divine nature and all the gifts and fruits of the spirit. This is the free gift of redemption.

> *"Whereby are given unto us exceeding great and precious promises: that by these ye might be partakers of the divine nature."*
> — 2 Peter 1:4

Transformational Redemption

This is a "Radical Transformational Redemption." It is grace at its finest.

> *"Therefore, if anyone be in Christ, he is a new creation; old things have passed away; behold, all things have become new."*
> —2 Cor. 5:17

The Pure Christos

Righteousness Consciousness represents the pure Christos, the Christ within, the Kingdom of God that is within you. The God within you doesn't know any dogma and does not connect through religion. God is not self-righteous.

> *"God is not a respecter of persons."*
> —Rom. 2:11

The God within you knows Sin Consciousness was overcome at the Cross and will have nothing at all to do with it. The God of your Kingdom is living in your precious heart, abiding in you. All that the Christ within you needs is for your heart to be open.

Opening the Door to Your Heart

How do we get our hearts to open? We know this much: Faith worketh by love. Faith worketh by love, my fellow humans, the love that is in your heart. When your heart is open, you have the love of God. You can feel it. It is real. You have the Christos. Righteousness Consciousness is the very opposite of religion. Religion wants you to work it. God wants you to:

> *"Seek ye first the Kingdom of God and His righteousness and all else will be added on to you."*
> —Matt. 6:33

Chapter 3

Dogma and Guilt

Religion is about dogma and law. Religion wants you to be in mind control thinking, in constant worry, and in doubt and fear. Its purpose is to keep you in works, guilt, doubt, and condemnation. It strives to put before you the stumbling block of doing it for yourself (the old self) with the old self leading and controlling your actions, desiring always to distract you from the natural leading of your Christos. Religion says you must strive to be better, you must do everything right, and you must obey the religious laws to have more spirit power. It wants to convince and manipulate you to believe you must submit to its laws. Religion wants you to fix yourself—to get that which you already have and already are in your innate spiritual essence.

Religion has many demands—it asks you to tithe more, pray more, study more, meditate more, go to church more, be a better you, it infers that you are not good enough! The opposition of your essence wants you to be all wound up in self-effort, stressed out in works, focused on anything and everything but the faith that worketh by love. You are love and God is love. God is not moved by dogma or teachings—the only thing that will evoke a move of God in your life is your faith, the faith that you already have. You have faith for everything you need—it is in your Kingdom, the very Kingdom within you, in your Christ, in your hope and glory. As you learn to use your faith to step out into destiny and stand against deception and dogma, your faith will be activated. You will be in agreement with your Holy Identity. This is the new creation, the new creature in Christ.

> *"But we all, with open face beholding as in a glass the glory of the Lord, are changed into the same image from glory to glory, [even] as by the Spirit of the Lord."*
> —2 Corinthians 3:18

New Creation Freedom

The new creation is about the fruit of love and faith. Grace is by faith, and faith worketh by love. Perfect love casts out fear. There you have it. All that other stuff, all the add-ons of the law, is mostly the Impostor's distraction to keep your heart closed and in confusion. You could be out dancing, hiking, making a predestined connection, living, and partaking of life and love everywhere you go, your heart opening fully to your innate, radical joy. You could be listening to beautiful music, making a new friend, accepting an opportunity that has the possibility to open your heart by simply giving your love.

The Impostor is a time waster, a spiritual buzzkill. Choosing your thoughts is a living prayer, the walking Word, without law. When you walk in liberty, you will begin to notice that your heart is opened in divine peace, love, and joy. An open heart is a heart that has been expanded by faith, through the process of life and the fruits of your spirit.

We have been oppressed and instructed by Sin Consciousness to "not live," which is the nature of the law of sin and death. Death is not living. Trying to live in the law, living in fear contractions and oppressions, is spiritual death. This is the very law you were redeemed from by love.

Mind Control Territory

All of the Impostor's manipulations are a predetermined plan to keep us in our heads and therefore in the territory of the fear mind, to encourage the thinking, planning, doubt, worry, and concern of the Impostor: to arrest our life force. The Impostor wants your heart slammed in repression, for this inner oppressor knows that if it can seduce you away from your authentic connections, your joy and your love, you will be lost in doubt and will succumb to mind control. You will not experience the release of your love that faith needs to work. Remember always that faith worketh by love, the love that you already have in your heart.

The Impostor is not trying to deprive you of your studies—in fact, it is encouraging your time spent pondering, reading, and being introspective. This is where it reigns. What good is divine love if it is slammed behind a prison wall in solitary confinement, oppressed in the territory of mind control—a heart with all its passions held back, by the quench of religion?

Perfect love casts out fear, yet the quench of oppression and repression brings fear in!

The truth is the Impostor has convinced many people, maybe even you, that they are a loser, a sinner, that faith worketh by works: by studying, by being very serious, by going to hear a lot of teachings, by staying home and feeding your head, or getting together with other folk who crave more faith, more of God, and then allowing the Impostor to lead, in discussions about works, debating scripture, paths, ways, and teachings—always more teachings. The Impostor only leaves room for arguing over who is right, who knows more, and who is holier—no hugs, no love. Sometimes we are deceived into allowing our divine fellowship, the very connections that are intended to embrace God's moment, and has the power to cast out fear, to bow to the self-righteousness of religion.

More Mind

The mind of the Impostor has many religions, many idols. Often the more we feed the mind; the more compulsive studying we employ to get to God, the more we get lost and confused in multiple options, new ways, and other people's revelations. Excessive input fills up our holy space, the very opening we need to hear from God. To receive peace and trust, we need to connect to the divine, to have our own revelations, and our own Godly direction. We need to connect to each other! We could be accepting, nurturing, and opening our hearts to each other, which would enable our love to be released. Instead, we often obey the desires of the Impostor and over-saturate ourselves with too many words. We become dependent on books, leaders, and teachings. This is the breeding ground for doubt and idolatry.

> *"Be still and know that I am God!"*
> —Psalm 46:10

Distractions

Anything you put above the leading of your spirit is a distraction to your holiness. This distraction can stop your ability to be led by numbing you to your innate sensitivity, to the prompting of the spirit. The numbness that you may feel, is your heart shutting down in anger, tired of being abused by deception. This is an attack on your heart. Years of this abuse can cause an actual heart attack. This is more than stress related. This is spirit related. This "attack" can be an accumulation of repressed rage, creating a block in an angry and disgusted heart, one having been deprived of authentic connections and expression for too long, a heart overwhelmed by too many words that are not true to its purpose.

Love, Love, and Love in Action

When your heart is open, you are led by God without Sin Consciousness. You are then led to focus on two things: the two commandments that are pertinent to the New Testament:

> *"Thou shalt love the Lord thy God with all thy heart, and with all thy soul, and with all thy mind."*
> —Matt. 22:38

> *"And the second is like unto it,*
> *Thou shalt love thy neighbor as thyself."*
> —Matt. 22:39

Faith worketh by love! God created it to be that way. God made it easy. We can then add "grace is by faith."

Is this beginning to add up? It is organic and natural. This error of interpretation is not the fault of people—I have been there many times, we all have, in utter innocence. It is a seductive trap.

Where Did This Trap Come From?

There exists in the old nature a generationally inherited Sin Consciousness. This is corruptible seed. This is what Christ has redeemed us from at the Cross, into The Perfect Law of Liberty: the gift of grace.

Translated

By one blood offering, we have become the new creation: The Righteousness of God in Christ, separated and sanctified from the old law of sin and death, and translated into The Perfect Law of Liberty. It's a done deal. You cannot do it better. You can only revere and honor the Cross of Christ by living large in love. This is true worship unto the Lord.

> *"But the natural man receiveth not the things of the Spirit*
> *of God: for they are foolishness unto him: neither can he*
> *know them, because they are spiritually discerned."*
> —1 Cor. 2:14

The Opposite of Sin Consciousness

This is not the limited salvation that religion represents. This is not a pie-in-the-sky hype. It is not waiting for a great afterlife hoping for a sooner-than-later death while you piously suffer here on Earth. Righteousness Consciousness represents Christ, His truth, power, love, and Spirit—hardly the evil perceptions of a condemning Sin Consciousness. Righteousness Consciousness is how you freely think in your Holy Identity. It is the exact opposite of Sin Consciousness and all the beliefs of religion.

"The Lord upholds the righteous."
—Isaiah 41:13

The Purpose of Dogma

The purpose of religious dogma is part of the Impostor's plan to keep you out of your power, to keep you in its mind control system. All of the Impostor's contrived dogma is a distraction to keep you from finding out who you truly are. Its goal is to keep your heart shut down, unable to feel your truth, your love, and your essence, unable to feel and respond to life.

Stuck in the Carnal Mind

The Impostor is trying to ensure itself that you are led by the carnal mind, trapped in the fruits of the flesh, the old creation, the one from which Christ redeemed you. The old creature wants to keep you justifying who you are not and worshipping false Gods in a religion that has very little to do with Christ Jesus. Once you find out who you truly are, you will begin to arrest (not receive) these destructive words of fear and doubt, the words of the inner Impostor of your identity. Once you make this discovery, everything in your life will begin to change to the way that God created it to be. You will be in agreement with destiny. This, my friends, is a word war! It is not a compulsive list of do's and don'ts. As your heart is filled with "your" words, the Impostor of your identity will bow to you. If you, my sisters and brothers, are bowing to it, you have been set up in exactly what the Impostor is consecrated to do: to create an idol.

> *"And what agreement hath the temple of God with idols for ye are the temple of the living God; as God hath said, I will dwell in them, and walk in them; and I will be their God, and they shall be my people."*
> —2 Corinthians 6:16

Idols of Mind Control

The Impostor wants you to bow to it and then it wants you oppressed in idolatry. Mind control is an idol! It is more subtle than the idols of ancient times, when people were bowing to external idols, like cows or gold. This one is much harder to see because it is the idol within, the voice of deception, the voice that may be speaking to you, right here and now, today. This voice may be trying to talk you out of reading or hearing this material. Religion, my brothers and sisters, is an idol. It is exactly what Jesus came to remove from this Earth: an idol that is predestined to keep you stuck in your carnal mind, deep in egocentric interpretations, in the teachings of man, and it is without the love of God. If this sounds far-fetched, look around you and perceive what has happened to many churches: people are walking away, disgusted, abused, and unhealed. They are not running away from Jesus—they are running away from the self-righteous limitations of hatred and religion. Many ministers are leaving their positions and are searching for a more authentic representation of Christ.

Hear the voices of believers around you. Who is speaking? Do you hear words of grace and liberty? Or are you hearing words about sin, words about always trying to overcome sin? Redeemed people focus on sin as if it is a Holy focus. Many good hearts are wounded and confused, yet confusion is not a fruit of God but the fruit of Sin Consciousness.

Right here and now in this divine new moment, you are beginning to distinguish, and thereby extinguish, this compromised Impostor-prophet from your Divine Consciousness. You are separating it from your God-given inherited mind, your holy DNA, the seed and mind of Christ. Your mind is being renewed to your Holy Identity.

Chapter 4
The Impostor and Religious Christianity

The Impostor has used and abused much of the existing church that many wonderful people attend. These are intelligent believers with available faith and great hearts. These are people who deeply love God and want desperately to have more of a divine consciousness in their lives. It is their greatest desire. They are people with faith—the faith that God has purposed to be directed to destroy the works of the Impostor, and to bring all of its misrepresentations under subjection. All that beautiful and Godly faith could be partaking in God's plan, in His divine nature. This Holy faith is more than able to, and is called to, contribute to an exposing of this anti-Christ con. Notice that "con" is the first three letters of condemnation. Also notice that the Impostor could be considered an "In-postor," or the Impostor within…

Christians Deceived by the "In-postor"
Many people, however, have been temporarily beguiled and instead of opposing Sin Consciousness and calling it out, as Christ did, these deceived, innocent, misled individuals are

oppressed and repressed by the Impostor's mind control teachings. The Impostor's teachings have infiltrated the churches and have been used to weaken and water down the truth of our divine rights and who we are in Christ. These teachings have been used to proliferate and entangle many innocent God-loving people into its deceptive plan.

Many Christians in religious churches have not grasped the understanding of who they are in Christ. They still think they are sinners, losers, and victims. They willingly and piously accept pain and illness, and often believe that God is the author of their Sin Consciousness sufferings. The Impostor is always blaming God.

Sometimes, these consecrated believers are taught that they are poor, helpless victims under a constant attack of the Devil. This "Devil" has become another God! There is a fear of being powerless with this "Devil," a belief that has become an idol in many churches. This alleged Devil attack and the fear teachings about this "enemy" has created in many believers a hypervigilant awareness of an external entity, an evil that is responsible for all their problems. The Impostor has created doubt in God's power and victory over negative forces and has been successful in creating another mind control idol, another submission to doubt, error, and victimization.

These erroneous beliefs often manifest in a projection, a looking out at the World through the mind of self-righteousness, the mind of error and fear. This is the very mentality that the Lord Jesus Christ came to and did overcome. When you look at your fellow humans and see their sin, you are projecting hate and Sin Consciousness. When you look at your fellow humans with love and mercy, and see their perfect divine spirit, you are seeing through the eyes of your Christos. Do not fall into the trap of judging yourself. Take your Jesus back today and rejoice! Your heart and opportunities are about to enlarge.

> *"We know that whosoever is born of God sinneth not;*
> *but he that is begotten of God keepeth himself, and*
> *that wicked one toucheth him not."*
> —1 John 5:18

Many minds have been blinded by the wicked sabotage of the inner Impostor. This is about to change! My sisters and brothers, you truly are the Righteousness of God in Christ.

Religious Churches

Many religious churches have innocently kept their followers focused on external evil. They focus on the problem "out there," the Impostor's twisted fear and projection of devils. Many sermons are focused on sin and tithing, and codependent "fixing" of the old nature. This "self-fixing" is the Impostor's will, to keep people out of a timely surrender and a personal experience of God. This is a compromise of your spiritual integrity and of your essence, a hindrance of light. This is not an authentic or even a decent representation of the Christ within, your Christos.

> *"For by grace are ye saved through faith; and that not*
> *of yourselves: [it is] the gift of God."*
> —Ephesians 2:8

Many misled believers have been oppressed and confused by this deception. Some have been repressed to the point of mental illness, often having been instructed to not listen to their own being, their own spiritual senses, and their own hearts. Many have had their spirits subjugated and have been led by mind control. They have become numb and passionless in mind control, their hearts slammed shut by this deliberate victimization.

The Impostor Quenching the Heart

Many suffering souls have not been informed that there is an inner counterfeit voice stemming from corruptible seed, a voice that might be controlling their life, mind, and thoughts, a voice that might be ruling and reigning in their own temple, destroying their health, and quenching their heart. This voice pontificates with a subtle direction of confusion and indecision, creating an unknowing alignment with the Impostor, thereby, perpetuating its seduction of guilt, doubt, and Sin Consciousness. Many have not focused on their God-given divine rights and authority, but on perpetuating punishment, as if punishment represents Spirit, the Holy Spirit, Christ, or the Great I Am! The Impostor has convinced them that redemption must be earned by good works, that it is not a gift of grace. This is the exact opposite of God's plan.

Mind above Spirit

Your authenticity or integrity are never a concern of the Impostor. The Impostor wants you to bow. This is its idol-like nature and manipulative goal and desire. The Impostor wants its fear-filled mind to run your life. It wants the intellectual mind to be above your spirit. The Impostor knows idolatry is the only thing that can temporarily disconnect you from feeling and being in the presence of an authentic God. Idolatry will render you powerless and wreak havoc on your body. Idolatry empowers the Sin Consciousness of the Impostor. Imagine that—religion itself is the problem, the disconnector, and the idol!

You do not want to allow any organized belief system to distract you from your God-given individual purpose. Your individual purpose on this Earth has within it the power of God.

Irrevocable Hostility

The definition of the word *enmity* is "Irrevocable Hostility." The Irrevocable hostility of the carnal mind will not and cannot submit to God. This might be worth a mention in the war between the flesh and the spirit, the inner war of the spirit and the Impostor, the war for your identity, your purpose, power, authority, and life force.

> *"The carnal mind is enmity against God."*
> —Rom. 8:7

When the spirit man thinks, he is thinking in Righteousness Consciousness.

> *"As a man thinketh in his heart, so is he..."*
> —Proverbs 23:7

Many Christians Today

Many believers are not living in this conscious state of a "Transformational Redemption." They are not in grace, the new moment, or the now move of God.

The Now Move

There is a "now move" that God is waiting for His people to encounter, create, and appropriate by violent faith. Many believers are becoming aware of this and are beginning to participate in God's vision. Many are seeing and confronting religion for what it is and welcoming the power and primal experience of their Christos within. Many are partaking in the divine nature and are inviting the Christos to move through them with love and power. They are getting out of their carnal minds and having an adventure with Christ. They are bringing the real Jesus back in a new way, a way of perfect liberty, a revival of divine love, acceptance, and healing power. Notice, I declared acceptance, not tolerance! Tolerance is the arrogance of self-righteousness itself. God does not tolerate you; he loves you and accepts you unconditionally.

This move is positioned in the spirit and is about to overtake the Impostor. The Impostor can easily be overtaken by the anointing of God in violent faith. The anointing breaks the yoke, as do the fruits of the spirit. Your spiritual fruits that are in your Holy Identity have no pre-Christ law. There is no law, trauma, or pain in your Holy Identity, no law of sin and death.

Righteousness Consciousness is predestined to reign on Earth. Sin Consciousness will be identified for exactly what it is: nothing but a bluff, one that was overcome and made a show of with the "Devil," and all that opposes the spiritual authority of Christ and His bride at the Cross. It was a complete and conscious redemption.

> *"And having spoiled principalities and powers,*
> *he made a show of them openly,*
> *triumphing over them in it."*
> —Col. 2:15

Temporary Oppression

Some believers have been temporarily oppressed and then reduced to bowing to the works of man, the works of religion, the mind control idol of works.

This is not the Christianity of Jesus Christ. This is the mind control religion of the Impostor! In this, there is the fullness of the Old Testament law.

The Impostor uses this lawful opportunity to create havoc, division, self-exaltation, hate, self-righteousness, self-justification, condemnation, blame, doubt, guilt, victimization, rage, intolerance, and a disconnection within and with others.

The Real Battle Is Easy

This is the exact opposite of God's divine plan. It is much easier to take your God-given control over your own mind and engage in the war to which God calls us: the war between the flesh and the spirit. It is much easier to step out by faith and confront oppressions, identify fears, gain power, and grow in the separation of flesh from the spirit than battling with forces that have very little to do with your current reality.

This belief and fear of entities outside oneself is another undermining of the Cross and an avoiding of the Word of God that declares, "There is no power but the power of God" and "Christ took the keys to heaven and hell." These external forces were conquered along with our Sin Consciousness mentality. The victory of the Cross was and is the restoration of your spiritual dominion. We as people of God "inherited" our position as the righteousness of God in Christ.

> "I will give you the keys of the kingdom of heaven;
> whatever you bind on Earth will be bound in heaven, and
> whatever you loose on Earth will be loosed in heaven."
> — Matt. 16:19

It is much easier to share our love—the goodness of Christ—than to focus on and perceive demons and evil in everyone. This has been interpreted by the recipients of such thoughts, as their being condemned and undermined. Because of these judgmental perceptions, the religious church people are often perceived as self-righteous.

Undermining words have even snuck into well-meaning prayer. Yes, the Impostor has gotten into our prayers. The spirit prays the truth of its nature, in agreement and gratefulness to God as a healed person, as a loving person with divine rights. When you pray from Sin Consciousness, you are agreeing with doubt and fear, and you are actually praying the problem in.

We do not get power from "learning" or from studying how to pray, but from changing our perceptions to spiritual mindedness. This is a perceptual transformation. Righteousness Consciousness is an inside job.

Prayer has often become another mind control teaching focused on negativity and the problems of other people. When we begin to focus on our own thoughts and separate our own consciousness from Counterfeit Consciousness to Righteousness Consciousness, to be who we truly are, we will be expressing our true authority and power.

"A double minded man is unstable in all his ways."
—James 1:8

Think on These Things...

"Finally, brothers and sisters, whatever is honorable, whatever is just, whatever is pure, whatever is lovely, whatever is commendable, if there is any excellence, if there is anything worthy of praise, think about these things."
—Phil. 4:8

You cannot walk away from religion by deciding you are no longer going to attend a religious church. That is a good step of integrity and faith. However, religion is utter unconsciousness, and you must choose to have your consciousness transformed, a process of sanctification, and an ongoing consecration to a separation from the old creature, which you are not. Only God can raise your consciousness to His. He does this by faith, revelation, and the regeneration power of the Holy Spirit. He does not do this by church attendance or tithing. Jesus is not religion! As a matter of fact, removing religion from the Earth, and destroying the works of the devil was exactly what Jesus was purposed to and fully accomplished with His victory at the Cross. With this understanding, it becomes clear why the Impostor is so dedicated to bringing back these conquered negative influences.

> *"Always striving but never coming to the truth."*
> —2 Tim. 3:7

Chapter 5
The Master of Your Temple

Let me be absolutely clear: However, or whatever, you believe, one part of you is being brought under subjection, one is the master, and one is the slave.

The master, the authentic spirit person, lives abundantly, *sans* guilt, in divine health, love, and joy.

> *"Being filled with the fruits of righteousness, which are by Jesus Christ, unto the glory and praise of God."*
> —Philippians 1:11

The Flesh Is a Victim

The slave (the flesh) is a victim, condemned, led by man, and always striving, forced to bow to the desires of others. It is a going-along mindset, a "not making waves" mentality. The victim is compromised and repressed in doubt, rage, anger, grief, sadness, confusion, passivity, pain, and despair. The emotion of despair is felt by the heart when it bows to the flesh. Ongoing despair is an ongoing compromise, a moving in a wrong direction. Re-direction is light years better than a verbal repentance. The spirit corrects the error and moves on in joy.

Your Holy Identity

> *"For we know that our old self was crucified with him so that the body ruled by sin might be done away with, that we should no longer be slaves to sin because anyone who has died has been set free from sin."*
> —Rom. 6:6

When I suggest that we are dead, I am declaring that we are dead to the ways of the flesh, the intentions of Sin Consciousness, the Impostor's ego mind. I state that we have separated our thoughts and actions from the carnal mind's vain imagination, and that we are able to identify who we are not.

As a slave (victim), the joy and fruits of the spirit have often been relinquished to the flesh. This is about to change. In fact, this is changing now, with you, in you, as you are coming into agreement with your Holy Identity. You do not have to strive to receive this impartation. The authenticity of this prophetic material has power to create a separation, a natural sanctification, a dividing asunder of flesh from spirit. It brings neither examinations nor wondering—it either will or it will not. The proof will be in the change of your consciousness. You will either experience more power over your mind, less anxiety, more faith, more hope, more clarity, or you will not. Trust how you feel in the next couple of days. Are you being inspired?

Begin to re-build trust in who you are and how you feel. The spirit knoweth all things. Trusting your true self is the mortification of doubt and condemnation.

Section I: Your Holy Identity

"But God hath revealed unto us by his Spirit: for the Spirit searcheth all things, yea, the deep things of God."
—1 Cor. 2:10

Your Position Is Your Weapon

More powerful than any lesson you can learn, stronger than even your personal purpose and destiny; stronger than fire, floods, and tidal waves, than the stars, the moon, the sun, and the sky; more powerful than any force on Earth is the power of the finished work of the Cross of Christ over your flesh, and over the Impostor of your identity.

This is your weapon over your mind and your body. You will have to be assured of this fact in your heart—your spirit is already assured. You will need to put your faith in the finished works of the "Cross of Calvary" in order to apprehend the authority of God over the old creature. This is how you will maintain your Holy Identity. This is how you will appropriate your authority over the deceptions and the wiles of the old creature. This is how you will undo any damage or illness in your body, mind, and life that the Impostor has created with its illusions. This is how you will assert and take back your divine rights and power from the counterfeit of your identity.

This sanctified and empowered identity is by "position," not by your works, not by church, and certainly not by religion. Your God-given grace, redemption, and position are free gifts to you, the spirit person, who you are in your true identity as the Righteousness of God in Christ. This is called "Righteousness Consciousness," a pure path to Christ, the path of the "Christos" *sans* religion.

Love God. Love your neighbor… Faith worketh by love, and grace will follow, for grace is by faith. When you step out in your faith, your essence will reveal to you the direction of your next purpose, God's plan through revelation. It will be released from your own beautiful open heart. God created a fool-proof, simple, organic system to love, to enjoy life, to stay healthy, and to prosper. God is not punishing you or creating havoc in your life. You are being opposed by the Inner Impostor of your identity, no more, no less. Sin Consciousness (which was conquered at the Cross) is trying to make a comeback through your carnal mind, through the old creature's delusional realities and triggers that no longer belong to you. Thankfully, these are thoughts that you can choose not to agree with.

Grace Is by Faith

If you have not said the religious prayer of asking Christ into your heart, if you have not been baptized in a pool of water, if you feel you do not have a relationship with God at this time, or if you do not go to a church, if you are de-churched, you are in a perfect place for a divine encounter. If you are considering leaving your faith behind, if you feel you are not making a connection to God, if you are not "born again" in a ritualistic sense or ceremony, if you are not considered "saved" by church folk or leaders, if you are being judged because of your lifestyle or sexual preference, or if you truly "don't get it" about the Cross, no worries, I didn't either.

There are many people in the church who are not authentically connected to God, although they would love to be. However, the Impostor has blocked their hearts with too many rules and "have to's," too many "must do's," "before's," and "only then's." These religious, Old Testament rules are often blocking many precious hearts and using "con"-demnation to keep them out and oppress them from their own Kingdom—the one inside themselves—the one Christ Himself resides in! You cannot get there through Sin Consciousness. It is a trap. If you think about it for a moment, it is ludicrous.

The Real Sanctification

I guarantee you with all my heart, as a prophet and scribe of the living God, one who God brought back from a medical death sentence and resurrected and redirected to divine health, without any religious laws; as one who is still standing twenty years later, with no lingering pains, no symptoms, colds, or flus, no special diets, hormones, pills, no illnesses, or doctors, this way of healing has been tried, tested, and true! I believe as you begin to arrest and identify the Impostor's decisions and thoughts, and as you begin to separate yourself from them, you will have a personal encounter with God. That is the real sanctification; that is what is vital to a walk with God; that is what is important to God. As you stop receiving the deceptions and illusions of the Impostor and are able to identify and recognize the lies, guess who is there? Hello God. Hello Christ within.

Your Holy Identity

> *"The Kingdom of God is within you."*
> —Luke 17:21

You will not discover God in religion, but within yourself and your own precious heart. Arresting your deceptive thoughts and beliefs is surrender. God will embrace this decision. Surrender is faith in action, not just a verbal declaration, but a literal undoing of error, a laying down of the idol of mind control and all its allies of deception.

> *"Inherit the Kingdom of God prepared for you from the foundation of the world."*
> —Matt. 25:34

> *"Inheriting" is not a ritualistic behavior.*
> *There are no works in inheriting.*

> *"God lighteth every man who came into the world."*
> —1 John 1:9

All of the attributes and fruits of the spirit that are often promised to be attained from ritualistic prayer and works become oppressed by the agenda of religion. You are now, always were, and always will be, a child of God. Unless you arrived here via alien transportation, I am talking to you, without human exception. In the depth of your heart, you know what I am saying is true. This is the deep calling the deep to encounter a loving God, to come out of the shallow waters of works, ritualistic teachings of man and religion, to embrace the reality of a spiritual being-ness.

I Who Had Nothing

I had nothing in Christ. My mother was Jewish, and I could not even say the "J word" (Jesus) without choking. It does not matter; you are reading truth and your heart is predestined to receive it. Your eternal spirit will resurrect and be empowered by truth, not formality and ritualism. The Lord truly discourages ritualism as simply another Impostor idol, a mind control jam. You are already way ahead without religion. I was way ahead by having nothing, no religion. I did not have to undo all of the religious misinterpretations and hype, a perpetual bowing to the law. I had plenty of my own bows to keep me busy. I had doctors, serious co-dependency issues, and psychological concepts. However, I had one less huge egg to fry: ritualistic religion, Sin Consciousness, at its finest. If you have less dogma, my brothers and sisters, you are more available to a God who is a spirit; you are traveling the shortcut to a rapid and graceful transformation in Christ. Hallelujah!

I was born again by a revelation, a God-revealed impartation, a personal experience—not by pastors or by prayer, but by Jesus and the Word of the Holy Spirit, Jesus. My revelation, my born-again experience, was my personal predestined word of my spirit's purpose, written in my heart before the foundation of time, and it became my purpose, my healing, my mission, and now this very book! It was a personal revelation, a word of destiny, released in my heart, alone in my living room; it was an appropriate and purposed moment in time, as yours is meant to be. It had the authentic power to resurrect me into spiritual zeal and exuberance. It was real.

Down and Out

If you are ill, disgusted, or addicted to anything—people, food, alcohol, drugs—you are in a privileged position to step out and experience your Holy Identity. If you are ill and at death's door, you are positioned for a miracle; you have nothing to lose, just as I had nothing to lose. You are available to fall on the grace of God and appropriate your divine rights. You can enjoy a miraculously rapid recovery. You have hit the Impostor's rock bottom. This is a one-way ticket to resurrection power. You are now, right now, learning to stand against fear and deception. Your essence has new hope.

Chapter 6
Enforcing Your Spiritual Identity

To be victorious in the identity battle, we must gain a deeper understanding of the gift of grace and define transformational healing. We must come out of the misconstrued interpretations of a simplified religious Cross and realize it was an all-inclusive Cross, a healing opportunity for all humanity and, simultaneously, a very personal healing, a Cross without limitations, a demonstration of a God-given Holy Identity, of eternal spirit conquering matter even unto death.

As Christ was resurrected over His flesh, over mortality, so will you be by and in Christ, over your flesh, over the carnal mind of man, and into your spiritual power and identity.

Without this knowledge and corresponding stand, you will be disempowered in the battle between the flesh and the spirit—the battle that you are here on Earth to win.

"For by one blood offering, He has perfected forever them that are sanctified."
—Hebrews 10:14

You are perfected, able to be separate (sanctified) from religion and from all worldly mentalities and victimizations, to be your essence. You are perfected by your inheritance.

What Does This Mean to You?
What did the Cross do for you as an individual? How can this gift that created a separation, a dividing asunder of soul and spirit, manifest fully in your life today? How can this gift of grace create for you the healing of your body, mind, addictions and disease, the healing of everything without exception?

> *"When you were dead in your sins and in the uncircumcision of your flesh, God made you alive with Christ. He forgave us all our sins, having cancelled the charge of our legal indebtedness, which stood against us and condemned us; he has taken it away, nailing it to the cross."*
> —Colossians 2:13–14

I have wonderful news for you...

Your Spirit Is Healed!
Who you are, in your Holy Identity, is already healed. All healing is the same. Your quest will now intuitively change from a religious victim's stance, a cry of "help me Lord," to a spirit's and heart's burning desire to have more of who you are. Your supplication will change... "I want to experience my healed position, as a spirit being and agree with my God. I want to personally appropriate and manifest a 'Radical Transforma-

tional Redemption' and gain more freedom over mind control, religion, and the Impostor's con job of illness. I am excited to grow by faith. Show me my Lord. I ask only that you direct me to the territory I am to overcome."

You will get God's direction and attention with that request. This will be a request from your heart, not the Impostor's manipulative mentality.

Done Deal

This all-encompassing healing that was finished at the Cross was given to you, the spirit person, not you, the seed of the generational flesh. That is the key to your stand. We all are two people: old creature and new creation, flesh and spirit. Your spirit is already healed—done deal—and any contrary evidence is the Impostor itself creating lying symptoms, which you are learning to deny, stand against, and overcome. That is the very purpose of this book. This is not denial, but dominion. Spiritual denial is the Impostor denying your true identity.

You have already had a miracle healing. You only need to push fear out of your Righteousness Consciousness, and its corresponding lying symptoms, and all of the alleged illnesses, and the physical manifestations that you may be experiencing, will bow to you. You will learn how to do this before you finish reading this book. You will gain a new world-wide spirit family to stand with. We will all be radically transformed by enforcing our divine rights and grace.

Identification Is Your Power

The healing of your body and the transformation of your soul to spirit is based upon proper identification. Identification is your power, a weapon in the spiritual realm. To identify who you are is to separate your flesh from your innately empowered spirit and to be in your God-given authority in the moment. That is the real deal.

Separation and sanctification are one and the same. It is edifying to see sanctification with a spiritual interpretation rather than a religious condemnation. This is a big difference and a life-changing view.

The old nature wants to sabotage your dominion on Earth. It has a plan to overcome you. It will use your generational past—exactly what you have been redeemed from. It is very easy for me to say to you, "Take the new moment, apprehend it. Be here now." It is easy to say, "You are the chooser and you are healed…"

> *"The Flesh sets its desire against the Spirit."*
> —Gal. 5:17

However, I have been there in this very battle for long periods at a time, and if it were that easy, everyone would be enforcing their divine rights, existing in the moment, and would be healed. There would be no illness. What is missing, then, in the "be here now" bandwagon? You need back-up. Your back-up is your faith. Your faith is being cultivated right now—faith in your Holy Identity. Many people today want to walk away from God, from their spiritual image, from who they are, and fix "themselves." The power of your inherited Godly righteousness is through faith.

The Fix-It Self

This "Fix-It Self" is the very self that you are here to overcome. It is a natural desire to connect with God, yet often in this divine attempt we get dominated by dogma and mind control. Sometimes, all of our efforts are quenched by Sin Consciousness. It is utterly heartbreaking to want spirit and to receive the law. This is the consciousness you are here to mortify. We are here to mortify the deeds of the flesh. You are not here to exalt your inner enemy and to follow deception. That is self-exaltation! You are not here to be tossed around and be led by error.

> *"We are not under obligation*
> *to live according to the flesh."*
> —Rom. 8:1

It is most important, people of faith, that you take this land back as individual vessels of God, that you follow your purpose and the God-given desires of your heart. They were divinely imparted. God agrees with the desires of your heart.

> *"Delight yourself in the Lord, and he will give you the*
> *desires of your heart."*
> —Psalm 37:4

A Being of Love

Love is always God's plan, that we love one another. Love is a fruit of the spirit. As we begin to identify the fake, the "trying to love" while not really experiencing it things will begin to change. As we surrender this counterfeit, we become more of who we are. We are divine love with all the fruits of the spirit; we are the real deal, in our "Holy Identity." We, the people of this Earth, are more than able to do this. It is very difficult and discouraging to walk in Sin Consciousness and "try to love" while not feeling love. It is very easy and joyful to walk in grace and Righteousness Consciousness, as a being of love, as a natural vessel of love. Love is a feeling, a divine passion. It is not an effort of mental ascent or works. Mental "assent" is a subtle form of self-deception.

When the Eye Is Single

Our love is upheld by our spiritual authority. You cannot walk in divine love without spiritual authority. The flesh will trigger you, and the Impostor will create illusory circumstances and perceptions of error designed to close you off to your God-given, well-intended love connections. Your authority will keep your heart open and your mind thinking what you naturally choose to think in your Righteousness Consciousness. This is a mind that is focused on love, a mind that does not receive what is not of love, a Divine Mind that brings unholy thought under subjection.

Just being you in your true identity and innate authority means that you already have the capacity to uphold your thoughts above the flesh and identify deception. This is one of your vessel's job descriptions. This creates a sustainable love.

Chapter 7
Your Common Denominator Is Love

Love is the common denominator in all our hearts. We have all been given the same love. God is love. You are made in His image. There is no shortage of divine love. The struggle is not real! The religious agenda of trying to love is inauthentic and oppresses the perfect love that you already have in your Holy Identity.

> *"And hope maketh not ashamed; because the love of God is shed abroad in our hearts by the Holy Ghost which is given unto us."*
> —Rom. 5:5

Sometimes it is just about negating the old self by choosing to give your love, it is a faith and warfare decision. A battle you define is a battle you win.

I am going to share a story of how I had a God-ordained encounter, a personal experience of divine love, and how it is truly everywhere everywhere except in the mind of the Impostor.

In the midst of an Impostor conflict, I was led to see who I truly was without mind control, without relying on thought, and was privileged to experience a total surrender of the carnal mind.

A Godly Intervention

I was invited to a church event, a testimony service, to be given at a church in Los Angeles. I will never forget it. It was the July 4 weekend and it was very, very hot—a Santa Ana wind and heat wave weekend.

I was still living in Santa Barbara at that time and was newly healed. I was a babe in Christ, one who was not yet confident in her new identity. I was led to drive all the way to West Los Angeles to attend this service, which was a two-hour trip each way. I wanted to go to be in the anointing of God and to have fellowship with my brothers and sisters in Christ in Los Angeles. It was a city I had moved away from seven years previously, and one that I was told by God I was going to move back to in the near future. I had my near-death experience in Santa Barbara, a miracle encounter and healing with Christ. Now, for my next promotion, purpose, and growth, God was slowly moving me back to Los Angeles. This was a city where the Holy Spirit was more vibrantly alive and where there were some unique and very anointed deliverance ministries to which I was connected to and the Lord wanted me to become a part of. I was happy to be going home.

There was a minister in West Los Angeles who was going to be sharing a testimony about a visitation he had from Christ. He was a young man, a new friend of mine, whom I liked and enjoyed. He was a very young man to be a minister, maybe twenty years old. Evan had been raised to be a minister. He came from a long line of generational Godly servants and was a very dedicated, awesome, gifted, and unusual person.

I Sit Alone in the Back

When I arrived at the church, I did what I usually did back then, in my newly healed days. I was still extremely sensitive to many things. I was acutely sensitive to hearing deception. I wasn't sufficiently grounded yet in my new creation, in my new position in Christ. If I heard something that I did not agree with, I would experience doubt and confusion. I was not yet aware that I needed to watch and refute within, that I needed to not receive the Impostor's interpretations, doubts, or fears. I did not know how to hold my moment, my separation from the flesh or my spirit mind above my flesh, with my authority in Christ.

I had not yet required any authority in Christ. I had surrendered to God (step one) but I was still without spiritual authority—a more mature step, one that the Lord himself would impart through faith and experience.

I chose to sit alone, a little bit in the back, so I could keep my eyes on the door. I wanted a sense of the crowd-one eye on the people, and one eye on the exit. If I started to react, it would be expedient for me to get out as fast as I could. If I did not leave rapidly, I would often feel oppressed the next day. I would awaken in pain, experiencing a headache, confusion, and a loss of my identity. I might feel anger or anxiety, which would affect my entire body and energy. Needless to say, given all that, I had a retreat plan.

The Impostor's Plan

I began to listen to the minister speak, but something did not feel right. He was about to share his new "Heaven" testimony.

However, the testimony that he began to share did not witness to me. He was talking about an encounter with Jesus: how the Lord woke him up in the middle of the night, just the night before, and took him to Heaven (again), and how in Heaven, he and the Lord went roller-skating in the mall. They went roller-skating on all the three floors of the mall! This was his testimony—having a skate with Jesus at the Mall.

As I listened to his words, I began to feel extremely uncomfortable. I was beginning to shut down. I had my own words to consider, as the Impostor had begun to negate his story in my thoughts. The Impostor's thoughts went on a negative roll: *"Jesus took you to Heaven and what He had to show you was roller skating?"* Going to Heaven, to me, would be such a privilege, such an opportunity. I thought if Jesus took me to Heaven, He would give me a revelation, or show me my destiny. Why would He choose to roller skate, with Evan in Heaven?

Can I Get a Witness?

The entire story did not witness to me or make any kind of sense. I believed I had a very keen gift of discernment, and I was not feeling the testimony at all. I felt it was inaccurate and I was starting to react to it.

Another situation that the Impostor was using to trigger me was that everybody else there seemed to believe it. They were enjoying it. They were fascinated by it. They were applauding it. I perceived the testimony to be a deception and yet everybody else was buying it. I was not edified by this outcome, and my carnal mind began speeding up and talking fast: *"Oh my God, what's going on here? Am I in the world alone? Am I the only person that's seeing and hearing this, feeling this way about the skating in Heaven? Oh my God! No one else realizes this is a contrived tale, a made-up testimony, a carnal illusion."*

During and after those remarks, I continued to shut down until finally my heart was slammed in oppression. My breathing was constricted, and I had little energy left to enjoy the rest of the day. I began to look for the exit and plan my escape. I wanted to get out and cut my losses, so I would be sick for a couple of hours rather than sick for days. My desire to leave was born entirely out of survival.

God Intervenes

At that very moment, I heard a voice from deep within my own being. The Holy Spirit released a command, loud and succinct, unmistakably God.

"I want you to close your eyes right now, my daughter—can you do that for me?" I said, "Yes, Lord, I'll close my eyes." I was elated to hear from God. I closed my eyes and the next direction was exactly this, *"I want you to negate all the beliefs in your mind—just say no. Say no to every thought you have. Just say no to everything you think, just a simple no. Whatever the thought is, don't evaluate it. Don't judge it. Don't consider it—just simply say no."*

Your Holy Identity

I replied, *"Yes, Lord, I will say no."*

I said no to every thought that I had and continued to negate my own consciousness for about ten minutes, ten minutes of very slow, concise no's, *"No... no... no... no, no, no, no, no."* No. I said a simple 'no' to every thought. It was a negating of every concept, every idea, every conclusion, and every word, not allowing any thought at all. Not one. *"Okay,"* God said, *"good, very good."*

Then, God gave me His next command: *"I want you to do something else: Keep your eyes closed; don't open your eyes. I want you to simply say 'yes.' I want you to put your eyes and heart on me, and I want you to worship me. I want you to give me your love. Say yes to me; open your heart unconditionally to me."*

"Yes Lord." I opened my heart to God. I put my eyes totally on Him. I was not thinking. I was in my heart fully, worshipping Him. My eyes were stayed on Jesus, single-minded unto the Lord, praising Him. *"Yes, yes, Lord, yes Lord."* I found myself engrossed in adoration. This continued for another ten minutes—ten minutes of saying my yes, of surrendering to love, of worshipping God without allowing any thought to interrupt; pure, undiluted worship.

Suddenly, the Lord responded to my worship, interrupting it, *"Now, I would like you to open your eyes. Open your eyes."*

The Room of Gold

I opened my eyes and the room had turned to gold. It was illuminated in a Heavenly gold. As I looked around the room, I was aware that all my perceptions had been changed. I saw the room differently, and I could now actually feel the room.

There was such a heavy presence of the Holy Spirit in the room. The room itself had been transformed. It was the same room, but it was now bathed in a rose gold. It was a beautiful and illuminated bright rose gold. It was clearly God's gold and the only energy left in the room was a strong vibration of peace and love. There was a feeling of divine love in the room. It was palpable. It was so strong. It was even in the air, in the atmosphere itself. I was surrounded by the love of God. Everything was perfect in this room. Everything was magnified and intense—the color, the vibration, the energy, the love, even the air. A haze of rose gold love had covered everything. This was indeed a divine room. It was a room with a divine appointment and everybody in this room, including me, was exactly where they were supposed to be. There was no other place that we could be. I knew this. While I was there, I knew this. It was clear. There was no fear, no doubt, no questioning, just the magnified presence of God. Everything was perfect and exactly the way it was meant to be. It always was. I suddenly knew this in the gold room. I knew everything was always perfect, God-ordained, and everybody was always exactly where they were supposed to be at all times. It could not be any different.

I went into a little bit of shock, as one might imagine. I questioned the Lord, *"What are you saying to me? Are you saying that I'm crazy? Are you saying that I think I have a gift of discernment, but I don't have it? What I'm discerning is not true. I'm just judging people. I'm hostile. I'm full of hate. Is that what you're saying to me? I do not see things as they are?"*

I took a deep breath. I did not know what to think at that point. I mean, it was both good and bad: good that it was all perfect and there was nothing wrong with anyone, but bad in a way for me, realizing that I apparently had no idea of what was really going on. Then God spoke to me again, clarifying His revelation, *"No, my daughter. I'm not saying you're crazy, and I'm not saying that you don't have a gift of discernment, because you do have it and I gave it to you. This is what I'm imparting to you. There's a higher truth, a truth that stands over all truth, a spiritual reality, a divine priority."*

"You, my daughter, were looking at their deception, at Evan's deception, and I was looking at yours. There is another truth. The whole Earth is in a deception. Everybody here is often in a deception."

"A global perceptual contamination—that's what's going on in the world, that's what you're learning to identify. You are in the School of the Spirit. Do not take it personally. The only common denominator that there is on Earth to get out of deception is love—my love in your heart. Your common denominator is love." He repeated it. *"The common denominator is divine love. Love is what you must use here to overcome deception. That's your most powerful weapon on Earth, and that is the only pure, uncontaminated truth, divine love."*

I received God's impartation in a very deep place in my being. My spirit grasped it and understood it fully and went into a holy alignment with it. The rest of that day, I just loved everybody. There were no triggers, no fears, no limitations, and no reactions. I realized that everyone was exactly where they were supposed to be. They did not need to be changed; they did not need to think better or to be more or less than their current experience. I loved them unconditionally. I accepted them completely. Whether they believed the story, whether it was true, whether it was made up, or whether it was real, that was all irrelevant.

We were not there to hear the testimony; we were not there to get a glimmer of truth from man, or to learn something. Not that you cannot learn something—that is perfect also, but that was not the higher purpose of our being there in the "Gold Room." We were gathered together to love one another. It was a holy encounter, a stage of glory. It was a place to be where I could give my love, where I could be a blessing, share my divine love, and thereby be healed. My giving of love was the healing. My giving my love could raise my consciousness to God's. The idea that I had gone there to get something, or to learn something, was a deception of the Impostor, an attempt to shut me down. If I judged it to be a good teaching, I was elevated, it was truth; a bad teaching, I was deflated, and disappointed. All the "blah, blah, blah" was a deception of the ego mind to block my awareness, to create a dependence on circumstance, a dependence on people. It was all a lie; I had a different purpose. I had a higher calling.

An Intent of Divine Love

My healing was to go with the intent, to give my love, to be a blessing, and know I was getting more than I could ever receive. I was getting my own heart to open. This giving of my divine love had the power in and of itself to open my heart, and then when my heart was opened, my true identity and all its power would be released. I would win this round in the war between the flesh and the spirit. The flesh would have to come under the subjection of my love. In this round, I would not be shut down to life, to love, or to God. My next revelation, the one that I was supposed to get that day, would be released in this new moment by my giving my love. My giving my love would open my heart. My perfect love was casting out fear, and with it, the Impostor's vain imagination, and every high thing that would exalt itself against the knowledge of God.

> "Casting down imaginations, and every high thing that exalteth itself against the knowledge of God, and bringing into captivity every thought to the obedience of Christ;"
> —2 Corinthians 10:5

Giving with the Revelation

That is why it is better to give than receive. Giving with the revelation and understanding that you are going to give, to be a blessing, with the wisdom of knowing how much more you will receive, will change how you see giving. This is a completely different perspective than giving to be nice or giving because you are a pious Christian or attempting to be a good spiritual person in the works of doing good. In these instances, you are allowing the Impostor to fake it. It is better to confront and surrender the deceptive thoughts of the Impostor to God, and open to divine love.

When you comprehend this, you will have a warfare plan. You, as the spirit person, a warrior in Christ, will vehemently choose to walk in love, to apprehend divine love by faith, knowing that you have authority over these deceptions. You will give fully from your heart, with your spiritual discernment and acknowledge, that by the very act of giving you are lessening all your personal disharmony. It will be a giving from the insight of the spirit, a deep knowing that you are there to give, and when you do, you are then able to keep the Impostor on hold, its perceptions arrested. You will be giving with the intent of letting fear know that you are on to it. Let fear know as soon as you make your decision.

Be prepared for what may want to oppose you when you go to give your love. What is about to arise is exactly what happened to me before God corrected my thoughts: the battle with the carnal fear mind, the flesh and the spirit fighting for position. Agree with God. Perfect love casts out fear. Declare it to the Impostor with confidence:

"There is no fear in love, but
perfect love casts out fear."
—1 John 4:18

Declare to the Impostor: *"Impostor, I am casting you out. I will mortify you with my demonstration of love, I know that my divine love has all power over your fear."*

Go as the Warrior That You Are in Christ

Go to win. Go to be promoted, to take down fear. Go to get completely out of your old self, and to leave fear far behind. Go to war, go to mortify the deeds of the flesh, and bring the old nature under subjection by simply appropriating faith and love. You are about to encounter the best days of your life by being who you truly are.

True to You Is True Enough

Do not allow your enemy, the Impostor mind, to worry about what is true or not. Cast your cares on Jesus, thereby taking fear and doubt down. The Impostor's interpretation of truth is not the point—that is the distraction to your promotion. You cannot have the gain from a word of truth that you can have from love. Be it truth or deception, there is a profound fact, a spiritual reality, that you are here to give love, to stay open to love, with love.

You are here to win, and you can only arrest the battle by having the victory. Take your power back from mind control, and all the erroneous judgments of religion and the flesh.

Watch and hear what will try to stop you from your divine love. Don't pay attention to the Impostor's case. Do not concern your true self with the Impostor's opinions. Pay attention to what the Impostor will do to keep you in its evil mind spin, what deceptions it will use, and wait on it with awareness, a holy separation, a God-led detachment.

Here Comes the Impostor

Here it comes, all your generationally inherited arsenal of lies. All of your triggers and familiar spirits are lined up ready to roll, to battle you, to take you out of your divine love, to overcome you, to bring you under subjection.

It may sound like this: This talk is a lie. It is not true. It is not of God. I do not like what's going on. It is cold, it is hot. They look funny, they dress funny, they are fat, they are skinny, they are stupid, they are out of touch, they have no class, they are in a deception, they are old, they are young, they do not like you, they do not believe as you believe, they are broke, they are rich, they are Lutherans, they are Buddhists, they are not of God, they are angry, they are loud, they are not loving, they are New Age believers, they are Jews, Catholics, Democrats, Republicans, blah, blah, blah, blah, blah… You know what I am talking about. Your ego's opinion of what is true or not true is useless because its truth is contaminated by a lack of mercy. It does not matter what is true and what is not true, in the Impostor's hostile evaluation, because there is a higher truth.

The Stage of Glory

The truth is that you are there for you. You are there on the stage of glory, grateful for a Godly opportunity, to have your consciousness raised to spirit. You are there to give your divine love, to give your love as a vessel on this Earth as one who is fighting the good fight between the flesh and the spirit, one who is here to overcome the old creature. You are here to conquer, and your weapon is love. Love is the common denomi-

Your Holy Identity

nator of all Earthlings and of all humanity—and that is a fact. The only thing you can truly do about that as a warrior is make the decision to give your love. You are not fighting people. You are not fighting flesh and blood.

> *"For we wrestle not against flesh and blood, but against principalities, against powers, against the rulers of the darkness of this world, against spiritual wickedness in high places."*
> —Eph. 6:12

You are fighting the Impostor's Consciousness that knows this truth, which did not forget this truth, which has eternal memory, and which is warring you for the position of your heart. The Impostor wants its words and its thoughts to enter your heart. The Impostor knows that when your heart is open, you have divine love, you are in your natural position; it is who you are. The word of God is written in your heart. God has put the whole world in your heart. Do not settle for a morsel of truth. Take advantage of this primal blessing. The Christos will be released from your heart. You are Holy Ground.

Command the Impostor to contain its opinions. *"No, not today, Impostor, thank God not today! I am on to you—you do not speak or think in this mind; this is my mind, the mind of Christ. I am not here to listen to your insanity; I am here to take you out. I don't care what else happens here today because I care about one thing, and one thing only, my purpose of this day, which is to bring you under subjection and to get more of*

God. You will not take my love. You will not take my mind." The Impostor tries to shut your heart down with foolishness, judgment, deception, self-exaltation, self-righteousness, self-justification, condemnation, doubt, and religion, all of which are based in fear. It uses these fears to continue telling you that you are not who you are to beguile and convince you, that you are here for a completely different reason, perhaps to get something from a person, to get something from a teaching, "to get something," to get something to become a better you. If you are deceived into buying in for a moment, the mind spin will begin, and you will be distracted from your truth and purpose. Stand strong at the portals of your mind.

The Impostor's Wiles

The Impostor would love to distract you by dragging you into arguments and other drama and have you convinced into believing it is you, as its purpose is to have you entangled and in all kinds of meaningless confrontations, bondages of the past, traumas, and triggers. These are the Impostor's wiles. There are many. You can fall in mortal love. You can get involved in a codependency. You can endlessly search for spiritual truths. You can become consumed with judgment or resentment. You can get into trigger fixing. Triggers go on and on and on, but once you understand the battle, the real war, you will have power to separate yourself from the Impostor's intentions by using a simple, *"No, no, no, I'm not receiving any of your conversation, Impostor."* You can look at God and say, *"Yes Lord, I am here to love. Thank you, I agree with you. I am here to give.*

I am not here to get. I have. I am grateful, Lord. You have given me everything I need. I am fully equipped. I thank you for all that you have given me. I am grateful to receive more of who I truly am. I am grateful to be in my Holy Identity. I am humbled and grateful to be in your school, the School of the Spirit. I am here to look at my brothers and sisters, and to accept and love them. I am here to see your purpose, glory, and life in everyone. I am here to see through your eyes..."

I Had a Change of Heart

The rest of that day, I was enveloped in divine love and possessed by the Christos. I appreciated Evan and his teaching, whatever it was. I was not caught up in it. I was there for a holy reason, a divine purpose. I saw that I am always in my perfect purpose, and so are you, everywhere that we go.

We are gathered together to love one another. I evaluated Evan's teaching in a new way. I was grateful that he brought a reason for the gathering of our hearts, that he called a meeting on the stage of glory. I was grateful that God had used Evan to bring us together that day, to have the opportunity to love one another, to impart an amazing revelation into my heart. Yes, Lord, Yes!

Sometimes, the focus on a myriad of teachings takes us away from the deeper things of God. The deeper things of God are not of the mind. They are not of the head, but of the heart.

Why not just go somewhere knowing that we are there to gather together to give each other love and give each other Holy Hugs. Giving each other Holy Hugs and Divine love is taking our purposes away from the Impostor at the Holy Gate. Why not confront and disable the Impostor and perhaps expose it? Make agreements with your friends and family not to allow the Impostor to put you in denial of its wiles.

Your holy expression must be bold in the moment. *"Hello Jane, I want you to stand with me against deception. The Impostor is trying to take my love for you, but I'm not going to allow it. May I give you a hug, a Holy Hug? Let's get into the love of God together. Let's break the power of this deception. Let's mortify the deeds of the flesh. Let's go up to higher ground. Let's agree and demonstrate that we have the love of God for each other."*

Now that, my friends, is warfare. That is breaking the power of deception and opening your heart to God. After that enlightened afternoon, anytime I would run into any of the attendees of that meeting, even by accident, crossing a street in the middle of LA or shopping in a market, they would run over to me and give me a big hug. They never forgot me. *"Hi, Juliana, I love you so much. It's so great to see you. How are you? What's going on in your life?"* They were connected to me in divine love.

Your Heart Wants Love

What your heart wants now is love. Your heart opens through love. What your heart wants is for your spirit to protect it and to give it the love, its divine right, the holy love that it came to give and receive. You can accomplish this with the God-given authority that you have in Christ. That, truly, is the desire of your heart—the most important one. Your heart and spirit know that giving and receiving love is the fulfillment of the new law and will keep you in the Kingdom of God, and everything else, without exception, will be added unto you.

> *"Guard your heart with all diligence cause*
> *out of it comes all the issues of life."*
> —Pro. 4:23

Now that you know who you are and that you are in an authentic battle, you will be more than able to take your divine rights and holy expression, over deception and reclaim all of your love. You are not nice, you are not pious, you are not faking it—you are the righteousness of God in Christ, in pure and Holy love.

Chapter 8

You Are Not Your Body

The more that the Impostor's ego mind, the mind of the old nature has bewitched us into the unconscious realm, the realm of relinquishing our power, the realm of victimization, the realm of "soul selling" the more investment we will have in agreeing that we are the flesh. Our focus becomes more flesh and less spirit. With each willful compromise, our flesh gains more power and momentum to oppress us. Sometimes we may become so befuddled that we begin to look to the flesh to heal us. I know I did.

"If you mortify the deeds of the flesh you shall live."
—Rom. 8:13

Dying of Deception

I spent years seeking help for my physical body. I did not realize that who I am is not my body at all, but a spirit. My real problem was not one of a physical nature. I was out of my purpose and was disempowered by misidentification.

I was, at one point in my life, deceived by the Impostor into looking to the medical community to help me heal my body, to heal who I am not. I was finally diagnosed with lupus, a total immune system collapse, environmental illness, and allergies to all foods. I was seduced into giving up all of my nutrition. Doctors called this the "Elimination Diet." Piece by piece, one type of food after another was eliminated until I had no food left. There were none that I did not react to. I had so constricted my consciousness by deception and fear that I had become allergic to every food group on the planet. I eventually bowed every food group to the Impostor until I weighed only sixty pounds and was dying.

My Body Had Nothing to Do with It

I was dying of deception, not illness. I had been living in utter isolation in the Mountains of Santa Barbara. I had just been given a death sentence by my doctor, a good man who had done all he could do to help my body heal.

I had been sent to worldwide clinics, been detoxed and medicated. I had removed mercury fillings from my teeth, treated systemic candidiasis—you name it and I tried it.

Each and every treatment made me worse and brought more despair until there was nothing left to try. I was then told I could not ever recover. My immune system had degenerated, and my organs were beyond repair until finally, I was told to go home to die...

It was at this eleventh hour that Christ entered my living room and my healing began. My healing was to be a switching of sides—a sanctification of flesh from spirit.

God began His teachings by having me fully understand these exact words: *"You are not who you think you are. You, my daughter, are not your body. You don't have what they say you have, and every thought you believe, every thought you think, is a lie. Your problem is not what you think it is. You don't have what the doctors have diagnosed you with."*

Soul Selling

"You have a spirit of compromise! Your flesh has battled your spirit to total oppression. Your problem is a 'spirit of compromise' a deception of the old nature. You have to lay this idol down. Lay all the idols down. You have bowed your power to doctors, you have bowed your power to healers, you have bowed your power to beliefs of error, you have bowed your power to man, you have bowed your power to medication, you have bowed your power to food, you have bowed your power to mold spores, to chemicals. You have bowed your power to everything on this planet."

"I have made you in my image, the Spirit person, with dominion on Earth. I have given you authority, my spiritual authority, over your body, over your mind, and over your emotions; you have been deceived. You are always my beloved daughter, and you are always a spirit being. You are always the same spirit woman to me, for you are made in my image and likeness. You have been beguiled into giving your power away and bowing it. You have compromised your essence and your integrity. That's why you're dying! That's what made you sick, the bow. And you, my daughter, must take your integrity back. You have to 'undo' the bow. That's how you will get well. You will retrieve your power."

Medical Death Sentence

Needless to say, that little chat was a bit of a shock. However, it was better than the alternative. My alternative was bleak—I was dying alone. I weighed sixty pounds and was unable to eat any food or even wear clothing. I could not leave my home, and no one could enter. I had just been given a medical death sentence. I had just been informed that there was no way I could possibly be restored.

I cried for six weeks after my initial visitation from God, terrified and shaken at my core.

Then, thoroughly motivated and completely grateful, I began to surrender all that I knew, all that I thought that I was. Thought by thought, I laid down my carnal mind, my life, my false identity, and all that I had. All that was left after my soul selling was an incredibly humble beginning.

Then, and only then, when I accepted and agreed with this Word from God, did the healing begin. It was to be a walking out of deception, a confrontation of lies, beliefs, fears, and illusions. It was to be a demonstration of my authority over the Impostor's insane system of the world.

I was taught to literally bring every thought to the obedience of Christ. Thought by thought, I was instructed on how to slow down and surrender my mind, and even time itself, to the Mind of Christ.

> *"For the weapons of our warfare are not carnal but mighty in God for pulling down strongholds, casting down arguments and every high thing that exalts itself*

against the knowledge of God, bringing every thought into captivity to the obedience of Christ, and being ready to punish all disobedience when your obedience is fulfilled."
—2 Cor. 10:46

Undoing the Bow

My healing, my brothers and sisters, was about "undoing the bow." I could say it in a more traditional way to create a new diagnosis. As a doctor of psychology, I am able to say it in an acceptable manner. But doing so would just be more mind control, bowing once more to the perceptions of the world.

God was very direct with His words, and there was no mincing or watering down the real issue; I had to take my power back from every mold spore, from every chemical, from every food, from every person, from every doctor, from every medication, from every false thought and belief in my mind. This was the holy diagnosis and suggested treatment from the Great Physician.

Undoing the Bow

I had to take my power back from who I am not, the flesh and the idolater, to become who I am: the righteousness of God in Christ.

That is spiritual healing. It is not waving a magic wand, doing a bit of chakra cleansing, or doing energetic revitalizing. The right pill will not change your circumstance. There is no perfect diet. Food did not create your illness and it cannot heal you.

Good food, perfect food, macrobiotic food, plant-based diets, juice fasts—I have often seen the belief in the perfect food mentality create yet another idol, an additional bow.

You are not your body. You are your spirit in a body.

Your body does not control you. God can keep you alive, healthy, and fully functioning on breath alone.

There is nothing new here. A Godly healer will investigate what is going on in your life to find out where you have become disempowered, where you were held back, and where you were manipulated to bow, to relinquish your identity.

A when, who, what, why, and where you were deceived into moving in a direction of temptation, an intimate look at where you were oppressed into entering the denial system of the Impostor mind.

Spiritual healing is a deep and Godly examination of what is happening in your heart and life, a who, what, why, when and where you were deceived into moving in a direction of victimization: A where and how you were tempted to relinquish your integrity and were not true to yourself. Divine healing is an intimate look at where you went into denial and were then manipulated by error to bow your identity.

Healing is a de-victimization and the surrendering of your generational past.

Inner Healing

In divine inner healing, you must discern where the Impostor has deceived you into relinquishing your very essence and into giving up your divine purpose. It is an issue of the heart and spirit. It is a deep and holy investigation, a spiritual "redirection."

Living after the Spirit

"You don't have these illnesses," the Holy Spirit shared at another impartation. "Nobody has them. They do not exist." These illnesses are symptoms of the bow. This is not living in the Christos, in the spirit, in the anointing of God, or in the purpose and destiny of God. This is living for the flesh.

"If you live after the flesh, you will die. If we live after the spirit, we have life. We are life."
—Rom. 8:13

We are radically alive, integral beings with joy, peace, love, power, and health, divine health. I always had divine health. I had divine health even when I was dying. I was not dying of illness; I was being oppressed to a lowered life force by the bow, oppressed to death.

The story of my taking back my power from illness, and ending the bow, is in my book of my personal testimonies, *"Enforcing Grace," How You Can Be Healed by God.*

I was led to confront every food group, every chemical, every mold spore, and every energy on the planet by faith, with my authority in Christ. In the end, I was privileged to watch fear bow to me. I took it literally by spirit force, by violent faith, by pushing back all that did not belong to me. I appropriated my healing of lupus and environmental illness by bringing the flesh under subjection. I am not some super-being. I came into the Kingdom of God with as little as any human could offer and still be alive. Albeit, I was barely alive, sixty pounds, hardly ambulatory, no family, friends, church, or any support or back-up. I had Christ alone.

I now have divine health. No more relinquishing of my power, my purpose, or my identity to health concepts, no doctors, or blood work. I eat what I choose to eat. Most importantly, I have no belief that I am just my body.

Healing, my friends, is a "de-victimization." It is an undoing of the idols of the generational flesh and restoring our inheritance as the healed spirit person. We do this by the demonstration of our God-given supreme power, knowledge, and authority over the Impostor of our identity.

> "The Kingdom of God suffers violence and the violent shall take it by force."
> —Matt. 11:12

Chapter 9

Identify Who You Truly Are

I had to identify, as you also will have to, all of my mind control, medical beliefs, emotional, spiritual, and physical compromises to become the authentic vessel of God that I truly was, and that you, too, truly are.

Becoming who you are will require the intentional unraveling and identification of the erroneous perceptions of who you are not, including the compromises created by the Impostor of your Holy Identity.

This is inclusive of the generationally inherited lies, beliefs, and deceptions of your ancestors: deceptions of the TV, the news, medical diagnoses, and seductive words that you have received and have allowed to enter into your heart. These include the words that you listened to when you were in agreement with the "Impostor's" illusionary reality before you were aware and present to refute, deny, and rebuke them. These deceptions are words that are always available to disempower you, words of victimization and misidentification, words you have been taught to believe and have been incorporated into your heart and carnal mind.

Re-Thinking

Fortunately, the moment belongs to you, the "spirit being," and all your new words and thoughts are at your discretion. That is how the moment is appropriated. The spirit being is present to choose and to re-think at will. Hear, identify, and take your will and moment back now. You will evoke the presence and power of God. Angels will applaud you.

If you are unable to take your mind back by just re-thinking in the moment, stand up, arise, and rebut, loudly and clearly. Tell the opposition who you are. It is just thought, yes, thought. It is not devils, nor the boogeyman, nor aliens, nor the dead communicating. It is the old nature's deceptive thought and you are the one with the power to choose what you allow into your mind. The Impostor's thoughts are part of a Sin Consciousness, and they have emotions, beliefs, and a will of their own.

When you are feeling negative emotions on a deep level, a level that is pulling you out of your joy and out of the spirit, this is not you. Stop, watch, and identify. When you are able to stop the thoughts, the feelings will be arrested, and your consciousness will change from Sin Consciousness to Righteousness Consciousness, not by the denial of feeling, but by the denial of thought.

If you are feeling emotional pain or despair, allow yourself to consciously choose to "feel" in an expansive manner. Do not be afraid to go deeper into the feelings of the Impostor. Never allow the Impostor to back you down.

Never allow the Impostor to oppress your spirit or repress emotions that have already entered into your heart. Take control, *"Impostor, I am not allowing you to shut me down."* Enjoy taking control back from the Impostor's illusionary reality.

Tell the Impostor Who You Are

"Impostor, I am not afraid to feel your despair. I am not afraid of your pain, sadness, grief, anger, hurt, rage, or any of your feelings; I can feel as deeply as I choose to feel." Allowing yourself to feel fully in the moment will unblock your heart. Your back pain, migraines, and other physical symptoms of emotional repression will also disappear.

Go ahead and feel with vigor as you are reversing repression. While you are feeling, tell the Impostor exactly who you are and exactly what you are doing. *"I am not afraid of you, Impostor. I can feel deeply and richly—you don't block me or shut me down. I am on to you. I enjoy feeling, and I choose what I feel."* Often, as you cut through some of the emotional blocks created by the Impostor's thoughts and repression of feelings, you will begin to feel your true feelings of righteous indignation.

Your heart has a holy anger at this attack being received, and it not being protected. Once you have your authentic emotion, righteous indignation, you have spirit power. Tell the Impostor you are not taking it, and, as a matter of fact, you are doing the exact opposite. You are taking your power back.

Surrender Now

Beginning now, this is surrender. You cannot commit to Christ without first surrendering your thoughts. Anything else is just the Impostor conning you out of a relationship with God, often making a fake declaration of a consecration to God, an illusory lying down of your life. It is a counterfeit.

These fake declarations are putting the cart before the horse. It is religion. You cannot tithe to God, you cannot stop fornicating to receive gifts from God, or do good works to grow closer to God. If you have not surrendered your thoughts, your actual thinking, to God, you are literally bowing to the flesh. To surrender to God, you must lay down the idols of the mind. This is true holiness.

Thought by thought, within a week of doing this, your spirit will arise. You will feel better than you have ever felt in your life.

> *"Casting down imaginations, and every high thing that exalts itself, against the knowledge of God and bringing every thought into captivity to the mind of Christ."*
> —2 Cor. 10:5

The carnal mind is thinking in the past, in the future, and in fear and doubt, creating and manifesting ancestral victimization with every thought. Identify and surrender who you are not. The rest will be a natural progression of who you are. Your Kingdom is there in you—unscathed, waiting for you to claim it by throwing the Impostor out. God is waiting for you to come out of your illusionary misperceptions and deal real.

Overcoming the Curse of the Law

The generational curse in your life is the mortal DNA you came in to overcome. Your mortal DNA is subject to the law of sin and death, thereby the curse of the law.

You were born into a family that has provided for you everything that gives you an opportunity to wake up. This was not an accident; this was, and is, spiritual opportunity. Once you see it clearly, you can begin to separate yourself from the vain efforts of trying to work your problems out on the mortal level. This will begin to arrest the root triggers, the re-stimulation of your past, and the power of the law that exists in your mortal seed.

The Generational Curse Ends with You

You are the one that has the power to end generational victimization and corruptible seed, the seed of man, the seed of mortality, by rising up and being the spirit person with dominion on Earth. Yes, you! You can cut to the chase of resurrection power. If I was able to do it dying, at sixty pounds. You can do it in your situation.

> *"Having been born again, not of corruptible seed but incorruptible, through the word of God which lives and abides forever."*
> —1 Peter 1:23

The Familiar

As a spirit being, you are here to overcome your mortal family's ancestral victimizations. You are not here to agree with, condone, nor acquiesce to your earthly ancestors, your parents, their parents, your siblings, nor your aunts or uncles. You are here to overcome their unconsciousness and stop the hand-me-down law of sin and death from influencing you. You are here to stop the generational bow.

You will be triggered by your family until you are able to exist outside of your old self, detached, and aware of the triggers and the ways of the old creation, remaining sanctified and separate from your past. Spiritually speaking, you are here to die to the old creature, the generational law and its trigger influences.

> *"For anyone who has died has been freed from sin. Now if we died with Christ, we believe that we will also live with Him."*
> —Rom. 6:8

When you have detached yourself from the mortal seed, you will be able to love your family with unconditional love.

As you become aware and not allow your true self to be bullied into settling for less than who you are, you will be upheld in the spirit. You will be living in who you are and who you are meant to be: Your Holy Identity. Everything else can easily become the stumbling block of works.

The New Way

The way of the spirit has always been to separate yourself from who you are not. As a matter of fact, the old nature may have you running around, spinning your wheels, and using your precious life to fulfill its unmet childhood needs.

This seduction of the Impostor may be the very thing you need to reject: the dark root of your temptations, the essence of your denial, your unconscious thoughts that have the power to oppress you into passivity, opposing your true nature and purpose. The old nature is addicted to idolatry, victimization, and powerlessness. It sets its desires against you, and it will do the opposite of what might empower you.

> *"For the flesh desires what is contrary to the Spirit, and the Spirit what is contrary to the flesh. They are in conflict with each other, so that you are not to do whatever you want."*
> —Gal. 5:17

You will have to see it, feel it, and stop its habitual repeating and reliving of the negative past: that which is "familiar" to you. You have the power to do this with your authority and divine rights in your Christos. You will need the revelation of spiritual separation and your "Holy Identity" to overcome it.

Once you are certain it is not you, that these thoughts do not belong to you, then you can easily reject them, deny them, and thus not receive the ways of the old nature and its triggers and problems—in the moment. *Resist* in the moment.

Everything on this Earth is used in perfect synchronicity to remind and assist us in being who we are. We are eternal beings.

> *"A day is a thousand years unto the Lord."*
> —1 Peter 1:23

"A Rose Is a Rose Is a Rose"

Remember, always beloved, you are spirit. You already are your Holy Identity, your divinity. That is who you are. You cannot possibly be anything else. You are the seed of God. The Impostor of your identity's job is to convince you that you are not you. This fake consciousness is telling you that the Impostor is you. If you believe that you are the Impostor or have any identity doubt, you will have more resistance in separating yourself from its old ways.

Separation Power

Renewing your mind to your Holy Identity will give you separation power. It is not a one-time impartation.

The Impostor wants you to believe that you are the counterfeit of your divinity, that you are merely mortal, that you are not spirit, that you have to improve yourself to be you. The Impostor wants you to believe that you have to work at becoming who you already are. However, if you have to work at becoming who you already are, the Impostor has you agreeing with its Counterfeit Consciousness, that you are not spirit, not perfected.

The Impostor may be seducing you into a demonstration of works on its behalf, a going along with its deceptive plan, always trying to get you to want to be you (who you already are) or fix who you are not. It wants you to bow to a mental idol and oppress all of your spiritual wisdom and power.

Chapter 10
Who You Are Is Not Broken...Don't Fix It

This is the fuel to the Impostor's goal, to get you to display an unspoken confession—a confession of actions to put your faith in all its lies. It strives to create a demonstration of doubt by having you agree with a belief that you need to "do something," that you do not have what you need, and that you have to employ "works" to get it. Every time you agree in your own mind and condone any thinking with this "fix-it" mentality, you are shutting your own heart down, your own precious heart.

In the very depth of your unique heart is your Holy Identity, with all the love, authority, power, divine health, divine consciousness, and all the revelations that you will ever need. This Holy Identity is the road map to your destiny: perfect relationships and connections, and your purpose and prosperity. Everything that you need is already there.

> "He hath made everything beautiful in his time: also he hath set the world in their heart."
> —Ecc. 3:11

Your spirit and heart know this, and can become oppressed at any misidentification. Actually, this is the very definition of oppression. This feels like confusion and creates doubt, a feeling of having lost your way, out of purpose and clarity. This is deception received. Disagree vehemently!

Your heart may have repressed anger about this abandonment of its purpose and integrity. Your heart knows that this is a bow, a bow that makes it difficult to connect to God, to hear, and to be led. This is often the time that the Impostor might come in with a second punch and speak a little more doubt into your heart: *"Where's God?"* Sound familiar? Just notice...

Don't Fix—Oppose

There is nothing you can do to get more of you because your identity is complete and secured in God. You can only agree that you have it. You are a divine spirit and are able to oppose the Impostor. When you are opposing Counterfeit Consciousness, you are automatically separate from it. This happens the minute that you stand up and say, *"I am not you. I am my Holy Identity. I am the righteousness of God in Christ. I am the image and likeness of God. I already have everything I need. I have nothing to work out with you..."*

"That's who I am, Impostor, the new creation. I am fixed. I have become new. I am redeemed and I am not buying your story. I don't have your problems; I don't have your fears. I don't have your lying symptoms. I am free in The Perfect Law of Liberty. A Kingdom divided against itself cannot stand, and therefore I disagree with you and I stand against you. This is

my Kingdom and you have no legal right to it. This is my vessel, my Kingdom, my body, my life, and you will not speak into my heart. There is no power but the power of God, and you do not exist without my agreement… I call your bluff! You do not trigger me, and I am not available for your fears, familiar spirits, victimizations, condemnation, or self-exaltation. I am going into my next new moment by grace. I am going into my purpose and destiny. I don't bow. You will bow to me. This round belongs to the spirit."

Remind and Retrieve

The minute you remind the Counterfeit Consciousness that you are you, and that it is not you, you have created a separation. Then, you will be able to disagree in the moment. Word for word, you have taken your power back from it. You have gone from victim mentality to spiritual reality. If you are able to oppose the Impostor with emotion, with your authentic righteousness indignation, you will experience a change of consciousness. You will be transformed from flesh to spirit. You will have successfully divided asunder soul and spirit. Your life is about to change. You are now a warrior.

The Impostor wants you to believe that you are a lowly victim without any divine rights on this Earth. This is a counterfeit mentality. The root of this is Sin Consciousness, exactly that from which you were redeemed. These contrary positions (flesh versus spirit and Sin Consciousness versus Redemption) are in eternal opposition. Sin Consciousness was conquered by Christ at the Cross. Do not allow the Impostor to use you for its voice. It does not have a voice of its own. Without your acquiescence, it is powerless.

More Primal Authentic Power

Words you may choose to speak to the Impostor…

Hey Impostor:

"I think my thoughts, I choose my words, and I will be the only speaker in my vessel. I do not agree with you. I identify your trap. Now shut up." Appropriate your "Divine Spiritual 'Tude,' your "DST," more commonly known as "Righteous Indignation." This defiance goes a long way in the spirit. It is primal authentic power. That innate power with your spiritual sword goes all the way up to dominion on Earth. The Kingdom of God suffers violence, and the violent shall take it by force. Yes, by force, with your "DST." It is in there, in your Holy Identity, and you can choose to use it. Just stand up and ignite it. Start to express yourself by representing spirit, and who you are will rise up."

> *"The Kingdom of heaven suffereth violence and the violent shall take it by force."*
> —Matt. 11:12

Agree with God

This is Righteousness Consciousness: knowing you have it, not begging for it, and not trying to milk God for a little revelation or a tidbit of power through excessive prayer.

Section I: Your Holy Identity

Do not allow the Impostor to make your rebuttal a religious conversation. You do not need to have addresses of scriptures or perfect recitals. You need only know who you are and express your true identity any way that it comes out in the moment. The key is to not think about it. Just rise up and roar! You may paraphrase scripture, express your heart fully, your anger, and freedom. You may threaten deception, call it out, insult it, and declare over it. Hallelujah!

There was a time in my life when I used to spend all my time fasting, studying the Bible, praying, and praising God, until one day God changed my direction, with a declaration: *"If you have so much faith, my daughter, get out of the house."* It had become all works. It was okay in the beginning, when I was a babe in Christ, but the season did not last long. There was a moment when I had to let go of all my works and trust life. Walk by faith. Let go and let God. I have learned to walk into my healing services with nothing: no agenda, no Bible, no pre-service praying or studying. I would just walk into a room, stand therein, and then wait on the Lord. I have never been let down. Do not let the Impostor do God any favors by talking you into a lengthy preparation. Any agenda is not led by God, any notes or preparation is not God's moment. You are deceived into allowing the law to lead. Your anointing, and revelation, will suffer.

There is nothing you can do anyway, so let go. Faith lets go and allows God to lead. Let go and let God!

Section II

RIGHTEOUSNESS CONSCIOUSNESS...

"A Radical Transformational Redemption"

Chapter 11
Identifying Sin Consciousness

It is always the plan of Sin Consciousness to have you think that it is you who bows, that it is you who creates compromises and negative circumstances. That is what Sin Consciousness wants you to believe. That is its constant focus and predetermined goal. It knows if it can convince you its errors are yours, your "generationally-inherited flesh" will become empowered. The Impostor wants you to blame yourself, knowing if you believe you are at fault, you will remain defeated and victimized. You will live in an oppressed consciousness, remaining unaware of the Impostor's thoughts and desires, creating a denial of your spiritual reality. The Impostor will then proceed to use its perceptions to create opposition in your mind and heart. Your flesh will gain momentum. It will kick you when you are down, intensifying all the fears, doubts, negative thoughts, negative emotions, and body pains of the old nature. The Impostor has total memory of all the triggers from your past.

The Impostor of your identity will become magnified as it creates this oppression. Your flesh will be exalted and enlarged. The flesh will increase, and your spirit will decrease in its power and authenticity.

Your Holy Identity

> *"He must increase, but I must decrease."*
> —1 John 3:30

This is not your doing. This is an attack of the old nature through Sin Consciousness and its condemnation mentality, using deceptive "thoughts," which often tell you that you have fallen from grace and that you must suffer due to an error on your part: a wrongdoing, an accusation, an undermining of your well-being. Go to these areas where you are attacked and take back your peace. Take your identity back and separate yourself from all dysfunction. You cannot be moved, be tossed, or have disharmony in your being. The Impostor is calling your bluff.

As far as this deception is concerned, there is always something you did not do, something you must do, or something you have done wrong. Identify this line of thought as fear and pressure—not the spirit mind, as there is no breath in it. This is the voice of evil.

Identify that voice and silence it immediately. It is critical and it undermines the spirit. The spirit is always edifying, loving, and uplifting.

The spirit is light. In contrast, the carnal mind (flesh) is darkness, and it feels heavy. If you focus your spiritual sense, you can feel it and see it.

Musings of Darkness

This is not your thought. This thought is opposing your separation, opposing your sanctification. It is battling you for position. Remember, it is only thought, the thinking of the carnal nature, the musings of the carnal mind. It is not you. You are always the chooser of your thoughts.

> *"I trust in the Lord with all my heart and
> lean not on my own understanding."*
> —Prov. 3:5

Grace Rules

These thoughts are all lies. Your grace is not dependent on behavior—neither yours nor anyone else's. It is only dependent on the finished work of the Cross of Calvary. Your grace is dependent on a spiritual fact (a law) which does not change. The gift of grace has been given for this very purpose and, therefore, there is no shadow of turning.

> *"Every good and perfect gift cometh down from the
> Father of Lights and there is no shadow of turning…"*
> —James 1:7

You cannot be tossed out of your redemption—it is not possible. However, you may have doubt in who you are, and you may be unaware that you have an option to take a stand, and thereby you may innocently bow to deception.

You are entitled to grace. You are in a "Radical Transformational Redemption," one that will facilitate divine health and edify your divine rights.

You are in the School of the Spirit, often in the trial-and-

Your Holy Identity

error system of life, learning, growing, expanding, becoming more of your spiritual identity and more empowered with each lesson. Your deceptive carnal nature wants to deceive you. It wants to punish you for your growth, for being a threat to its survival, for having the divine seed. This corruptible seed wants to reign over incorruptible seed; its main focus is to empower itself and oppress you. This victimization is rooted in the mentality of Sin Consciousness, which is the law of sin and death.

You, the spirit person, cannot compromise. It is not of your nature. The spirit has the sinless nature of a Holy God. Remember this always, and force the Impostor to hear this word...all day long:

> *"The spirit cannot sin...it is not possible."*
> —1 John 3:9

Chapter 12
You Do the Talking

It is always empowering to consciously choose to speak, into your own mind, giving the Impostor a verbal thrashing. This puts you in the position of authority in your Kingdom. "Impostor, I want to inform you of a few facts. I am born of God, God's child, in His image; it is impossible for God to sin, it is impossible for His seed to sin. It is you, Impostor, it cannot be me. Impostor, listen to my words loud and clear."

> "Impostor, I am exposing your unconscious rhetoric and your Sin Consciousness and condemnation accusations. The Word of God cannot return void."

> "So shall my word be that goeth forth out of my mouth: it shall not return unto me void, but it shall accomplish that which I please, and it shall prosper in the thing whereto I sent it."
> —Isaiah 55:11.

"Hey Impostor, I am coming up in my full Christos,

divinely empowered to stand against your Kingdom. I am calling you out. I am calling your bluff. I am backing you down. All the things of darkness will come into the light. You will not undermine my Christ or my identity or position on this Earth. You will not make the Cross of Christ null and void in my life. It is over. Get thee hence."

"The entrance of His words gives light;"
—Psalm 119:130

A Spiritual Takeover

As your voice begins to overcome the Impostor's thoughts, you will begin to become energized. You will notice symptoms of deception (lying symptoms) and oppressions losing power over your body and your energy level. You will be strengthened in your body, mind, and spirit.

Every time you gain a little power over the old nature, the Impostor will desire to retaliate and try to regain ground. This is a primal battle. You have enraged it by taking power away from it; it will attempt to create a situation, a trigger, to seduce you into forgetting who you are. It always desires to steal your identity. That is what an Impostor does. It needs your identity to live, to survive, and to function. It has nothing without your agreement, which means you have all the control. If you find that when you speak to the Impostor, you feel a little lowered, a bit heavy, as if you are being counter-attacked, simply repeat yourself and speak louder until you arise, until you feel your Christos power, until the Impostor bows to your words. Use your holy righteous indignation to call its bluff. When you conquer the Impostor, you will feel an elevation—that's the Impostor bowing to you and you will literally feel fear cower.

These energy fluctuations are not bipolar—they are not a chemical imbalance. They are an indication of whose words are being received in your heart and who is leading. Who is running your life, the spirit or the flesh? Who is up to bat in your Kingdom?

The Impostor wants to blame you for its errors and oppress you. To do so, it accuses you of compromise, always attempting to shut you down by constricting your heart with its words. You may or may not hear its words. It might be an unconscious voice, a generational undermining, a "Familiar Spirit." The Impostor may choose to speak the same words that you heard your parents speaking, in your childhood, the "Generational Impostor." If you are not aware of this voice, an unconscious oppression is being created when you receive its perceptions without identifying them. You can become disempowered by denial. This can be especially prevalent if you have experienced sexual abuse, verbal abuse, religious abuse, or other types of severe childhood trauma. These denial triggers belong to the old creature. Soon, you will be able to encounter its deceptive words with a consciously chosen separation. It is always good to let the Impostor know you are not buying its thoughts.

Hey, Impostor...

"Impostor, I know exactly what you are attempting to do. I am on to you." When you feel you are suddenly tired, go directly to your thoughts and take control: *"I know, Impostor, exactly what your intent is. You are trying to pull me down, to oppress me, with your threatening thoughts. I will not allow you to steal my energy, my mind, or my life."* You will feel an elevation as you identify deception and stop it in its tracks. You are arresting a denial trigger in the moment. This is a very powerful meditation; this is the healing of your heart. This is you guarding your heart as the spiritual warrior that you truly are.

> *"Keep your heart with all diligence, for out of it springs all the issues of life."*
> —Prov. 4:23

Ruling and Reigning

The Impostor may be setting you up. As soon as you feel any oppression or any lowering of your energy in the moment, quickly identify this aggressive onslaught of evil and use your authority to reign. These energy fluctuations are the works of the opposition to your divinity. Identification in the moment is the separation from the flesh. Turn on it, and you will soon be able to divide asunder soul and spirit, with your own holy words.

> *"For the word of God is quick, and powerful, and sharper than any two-edged sword, piercing even to the dividing asunder of soul and spirit, and of the joints*

and marrow, and is a discerner of the thoughts and intents of the heart."
—Heb. 4:12

When you begin to acknowledge the emotions that the old nature is attempting to dump on you, desiring to repress you, these hostile feelings will become your servant.

These emotions are born of the flesh and often from the spirit of self-exaltation, wanting to overpower you with its rage and anger.

You can choose to feel them deeply and then choose to add some righteous indignation to maintain your emotional and spiritual integrity. Instead of becoming repressed, you will be expanding your heart with own your spirit's righteous indignation. Your holy anger has all power over the Impostor's mortal rage. Do not be silenced.

Your silent acquiescence is a bow to the side of evil. Get your "DST" your Divine Spiritual "Tude" ready to roll and roll loud and clear. Pick up your spiritual sword and attack. You do not need anger management. You need to take your power back from who you are not. Without emotion, you are weak in the battle. The Impostor rapidly accesses your situation and knows you have become repressed and oppressed. It knows you are down for the count. Any good warrior knows there is abundant power in bringing your heart into the battle. Feel to be real and to know what is going on. You cannot change a feeling by denying it—that is merely going deeper into the dark lifeless hole of repression and oppression.

If the Impostor has been repressing your heart and oppressing your spirit and divine rights since you were a child, you have a holy anger. As you release this anger with your spiritual authority and the expression of your Holy Identity, you will also release a lot of repressed anger that you may have accumulated.

As a transformed and renewed former emotional release psychologist, I can humbly conclude that this is a very impressive position and accomplishment. It is an offering of divine grace, an inner cleansing of light years.

Your Voice in Declaration of Identity

Your voice is a very powerful weapon against the Impostor's belief system. It has the power to resurrect and anoint your spirit. As you declare who you are, your life will change. Your heart will open as you speak these truths over it. Your precious heart has been oppressed in the wrong identity by having to tolerate words that undermine its reality. Your heart will be so grateful and relieved that you are no longer allowing the Impostor to speak over your voice with its oppressive and aggressive words, it will rejoice. Your joy will be full. Can you feel the excitement in your heart as you contemplate this switch of authority?

Victim No More

Your spirit will rise up and take over after a few days of hearing God's holy encouragement. In a short period of time, after you begin to declare your Holy Identity and divine rights, you will release the warrior within and gain a new authority and awareness. You will then begin to hear and identify the Impostor as it attempts to speak to you in the present moment, instead of the next day, when you wake up disgruntled, confused, with back pain, a headache, or the ailment *du jour.* You will not have to look back; you will gain the ability to recognize and separate its voice from yours and arrest its deceptions in the moment.

This is the moment of the spirit—God's moment of authority. You, the spirit person, will begin to control your energy, your day, your emotions, and your life. This is appropriating your "position" as a vessel in Righteousness Consciousness: victim no more. You will begin to look at the facts instead of erroneous and hostile perceptions of what happened. What did the Impostor just take away from you? Did you suddenly feel angry? What is its narrative? What did it use to distract you from your identity? Did it use a headache, a cold, a friend, a trigger, a mind jam, an oppression of your expression, an energy fluctuation? Did it attack you on your attempt to take a new territory or on a move of faith? What was the verbal fear threat? Many of these lying symptoms of pain and disharmony stem from unconscious thought. You must first identify what that thought is, "hear it," and you will begin to take back your day, night, friends, peace, health, life, and mind.

If you are able to feel the anger, pain, grief, rage, and other emotions in the moment, while simultaneously separating yourself from the Impostor's thoughts (its deceptive story), you will be sanctified from the tale that it is speaking into your heart and wants you to believe, and you will not be repressed tomorrow. You will never again have to awaken tired and shut down in anxiety or pain. You can win this entire battle in the moment. Not by avoiding what is happening in the moment, not by letting it go, but by fully being there feeling, choosing, and thinking in your mind simultaneously.

Feeling deeply without the Impostor's thoughts can also lead to revelation—you are actually unblocking your own heart. Then, you have the opportunity, to choose words of faith, your personal arsenal for your Holy Identity warfare. Thoughts are words. Your expression represents your spirit or your flesh. Get in the real battle; cut to the chase of dominion on Earth. It is yours to appropriate and that appropriation is inevitable. Why not now? God is not the creator of suffering or procrastination.

Renew Your Mind to Remember Who You Are

Renewing your mind to your Holy Identity is taking over your consciousness, thought by thought, and co-creating with God for your "now" and for your future. It is agreeing with destiny. You may want to consciously choose to begin to renew your mind to your spiritual identity. You will suddenly find yourself choosing to enforce your Righteousness Consciousness and your divine rights by grace. This is quite natural, for this is the way you were created to think, your divine mind and precious heart connecting to the Great I Am, commingling in the moment. As your spirit resurrects and expands in its truth, it will automatically and efficiently do its job. It is unique for everyone, and how we do it changes as we grow, mature, and transform. The spirit's proper position is high above the mind, watching and choosing, abiding in Christ, living in liberty, sitting in Heavenly places in Christ Jesus.

> *"And hath raised us up together, and made us sit together in heavenly places in Christ Jesus…"*
> —Eph. 2:6

The Spirit Is in the Moment

This is a simple and natural battle. It is the battle for your power in the moment. When you are totally present in your Kingdom, you will hear and retort, you will pick up your spiritual sword, and with your own words, you will be evicting deception. You will conquer in the very moment that it speaks, and you will soon be able to go into the battlefield of the mind, hearing and responding word for word. You, the spirit person, will be fighting against deception with spiritual fact.

When I suggest "word for word," I mean it is important for you to respond directly to what you hear; you must hear clearly to respond in the moment. Hearing and responding is not randomly spouting truths, affirmations, or memorized scripture. It is watching, praying, praising, and refuting with an awareness of every word. Take your mind back. This is Holy Ground.

This will make the Impostor of your identity bow to you! Do not underestimate your opponent. Use your eternal immortal wisdom. There is a distinct difference in the warfare of the moment that is present to nullify the Impostor's thoughts, emotions, and intents. It is of the spirit, not the works of mind control. Renewing your mind to the truth of who you are in the moment is not part of the religious agenda of the flesh, it is not the law. Instead, it is the pure Christos being released in you. It is higher ground!

Let's put some truths in your heart right now. These truths will return organically by faith when you need them.

They will come up and edify your DST. You can repeat loudly and clearly some spiritual facts to the Impostor. When you do this, you are announcing that you are aware of its game, and that you are no longer in denial.

Hey Impostor…

"Impostor, I want to inform you of some spiritual facts, flesh cannot shut spirit down. You are a mere bluff, Impostor. I have the power, the sword of the spirit, my authority in Christ, the regeneration and resurrection power of the Holy Ghost. I call upon it boldly."

"And take the helmet of salvation, and the sword of the Spirit, which is the word of God…"
—Eph. 6:17

"Hey Impostor, I am on to you. You will not exalt yourself above the power of God. I break down your strongholds, destroy your Kingdom by force and spiritual violence. Get behind me. You are not me. I separate myself from you. Your triggers, issues, fears, and problems are not mine.

They do not belong to me! How dare you pretend to be me, to undermine my inheritance and my Christ within. I am here to bring you under subjection. You

Section II: Righteousness Consciousness...

cannot shut me down—you are merely mortal, you are flesh, and I am spirit, immortal and eternal. I am the Lord, the second man from Heaven—you are Adam, a living soul."

"The first man was made a living soul: the last Adam was made a quickening spirit..."
—1 Cor. 15:45

"Impostor, you have no power over me, for there is no power but the power of God."
—Rom. 6:6

"Let every soul be subject unto the higher powers. For there is no power but of God: the powers that be are ordained of God..."
—Rom. 13:1

"The Kingdom of God suffereth violence and the violent shall take it by force..."
—Matt. 11:12

"The tearing down of strongholds and every high thing that exalts itself against the knowledge of God..."
—2 Cor. 10:15

"Impostor, I am standing strong, in my Holy Identity, as a vessel in the Kingdom of God—

Your Holy Identity

> *I'm bringing you down by force, by faith, and by violence, by my spiritual position in Christ, and my authority in the Word of God..."*

Once you learn to enforce your grace in this area and arrest these spiritual attacks and oppressions, your life will be much easier. You will be going from grace to grace, counting it all joy—*all joy!* And you will be laughing out loud everywhere, exuberant with irrepressible joy, the joy of the Lord.

Chapter 13

Familiar Spirits of Fear

If you are suffering from a spirit of fear that has you believing it belongs to you, or if you are listening to a spirit of fear speak to you, as if it is you, it can be very oppressive. It is far from peaceful, if you are afflicted and abused by a fear filled Sin Consciousness. A Condemnation Consciousness will always choose to shut down your heart and choose to poison you with a seed of evil that will punish you after each learning experience.

Triggers of the Past

This punishment is not of God and it is not acceptable. Bust the con (condemnation) of this identity undermine and expose the error of grace denied by the Impostor's setups and beliefs. The Impostor will set you up and use familiar spirits and situations to condemn you and shut you down. The fear of this happening becomes a trigger in and of itself: the "fear of" familiar spirits (triggers from the past). These triggers are generational conditioned ways of feeling and responding from your old nature's fear history.

Trauma Triggers Do Not Belong to You

These trauma triggers (your fear history) are not in your new moment and no longer belong to you. As the spirit person, you are now able to guard your heart, to speak your truth, and to handle every situation in your integrity. Your expression of your heart, your sharing your heart with others, is your emotional integrity, and will keep your heart open and your flesh quiet. Letting everything go is not a holy or spiritual attribute. It is fear and darkness, an inauthentic thought process, allowing the Impostor to push you down. As we express ourselves in our Holy Identity, and speak our truth with love, we are able to resolve all conflicts and confusion in the moment. The power of our integrity in Christ disables the Impostor and reduces its ability to victimize us and shut down our precious hearts.

Repression and oppression are the tools of the Impostor to keep us out of our spiritual aliveness.

> *"But speaking the truth in love, may grow up into Him in all things, who is the Head, even Christ."*
> —Eph. 4:15

Familiar Spirits

A familiar spirit is an old way, a going unconscious in denial. You, the people of the spirit, are able to express yourself with clarity and humility. You are not fighting flesh and blood, but spiritual wickedness in high places. You are fighting thoughts, both thoughts you are aware of and unconscious thoughts.

When you feel your heart is quenched or your spirit is oppressed, it is time for you to express your reality.

> *"For we do not wrestle against flesh and blood, but against principalities, against powers, against the rulers of the darkness of this age, against spiritual 'hosts' of wickedness in the heavenly places."*
> —Eph. 6:13

Identifying Familiar Spirits

A familiar spirit carries the old voices and behaviors of the denial system that you may have experienced in your childhood. It does not belong to you, the spirit being. You must be firm in your Holy Identity to recognize its presence. These voices of familiar spirits want to lull you into oppression and repression of your feelings. They desire to lower your consciousness and create a passivity so that they may steal your "now," your moment, your true identity and authentic expression.

Identifying, understanding, and being aware of these "familiar spirits" can be empowering in the battle. For instance, once you are anticipating what will happen after a victory, you can lie in wait for the attack, prepared and fully armed. Instead of wondering why you are oppressed, depressed, or undermined, you will be excited, enlightened, and a warrior in the battle. The flesh is always trying to mislead you and the spirit is always warning and protecting you. There are signs everywhere. Report, perceive, and express your situations from a spiritual perspective—from who you are. This will empower and separate you.

> *"If I be dead with Him, I shall also live with Him."*
> —2 Tim. 2:11

Once you have identified these familiar spirits, you can begin to separate yourself from them. By not allowing the flesh to bow to them, you can effectively slam the door on them. You have nothing to work out with evil's premeditated plan. There is no gain. You are already redeemed; move on in faith and soon they will all disappear. You will begin to push them back, with the demonstration of your Holy Identity.

> *"Not with enticing words of man's wisdom, but with the demonstration of spirit and power."*
> —1 Corinthians 2:5

God is not sending familiar spirits to oppress you. God is not sending the past for you to relive over and over again. There is nothing to gain from the flesh. God is in the new "now." God is sending blessings, abundance, and opportunity. Do not permit the flesh to seduce you into settling for anything less. It can cost you a battle. Remember, above all things, you are here to win. You are predestined to win: fated, before the beginning of time, to bring the flesh under subjection. You do not need to tolerate the abuse of a familiar spirit. These spirits are hypnotic, using their wiles to render you unaware, so they can steal your moment. It is the plan of Sin Consciousness to take your Kingdom down by re-stimulating your past on an unconscious level.

You may not hear the words, but you may still feel an energetic debilitation. Be aware and resist. Take over. These are not your triggers to fear. These are shadows of the past. God is here now, in your new, holy, sanctified moment. Do not give the flesh your moment. Stay awake. Watch and pray. You do the thinking. You do the feeling. You do the talking in your mind. Take over!

> *"If any man be in Christ, he is a new creature; old things have passed away, all things have become new."*
> —1 Cor. 6:16

Take your moment back. Take your holy moment back now.

The Old Nature is an addict. The flesh (the old creature) has an addiction to giving power away, to bowing, and to compromising to get what it wants. It is a victim! That is its nature and that is what it does. That is who it is and all it has. It wants to silence your expression. It wants to mislead you. It will try to pull you on its course, to toss you like a leaf at sea. It is not you. Your job, as the spirit person, is to reclaim your power.

> *"That we should no longer be children, tossed to and fro and carried about with every wind of doctrine, by the trickery of men, in the cunning craftiness of deceitful plotting."*
> —Eph. 4:14

If you know the areas where the old nature is generationally conditioned to bow, you can stay awake. This is overcoming; this is dying to powerlessness, doubt, and victimization. You can lay these idols down at the Cross of Christ. These alleged triggers and past traumas are the Impostor's breeding ground to condemn you and to bring your generational past, fear, doubt, guilt, and shame into your heart. Your heart has already been redeemed from these triggers. They are just calling your bluff.

You are in a Radical Transformational Redemption, one which includes the complete separation from your past triggers, traumas, and all your generationally inherited principalities. The Impostor will use these triggers to try to get you in agreement with its thoughts and emotions. It wants you to bow to its fears, to possess you, to become you.

> *"Stand firm in the liberty in which Christ hath set you free: You are no longer entangled with the yoke of bondage."*
> —Gal. 5:1

Chapter 14

The Trigger Is the Bow

I am going to share a profound revelation with you, and as this divine truth is being imparted into your heart, your spirit will be empowered to remain sanctified and divinely separated from the evil intentions of the Impostor. Let this sink into your heart, mind, and spirit: there is no such thing in the spirit as trauma or triggers—they do not exist. Jesus is an incredible psychologist.

If you are not deceived by a familiar spirit to go unconscious in the Impostor's denial system, or its preconceived setup, there is no trigger. There is no trigger if there is no fear of the trigger. The Impostor uses a familiar spirit to overcome you, seducing you out of your "position" as the righteousness of God in Christ, to create a "bow." It wants to create a compromise. Remember, the Impostor's nature is that of a compromiser—that is what it is. It wants you to go unconscious and be seduced to a bow. A temptation, a re-stimulation, or a fear trigger has the ability to make you passively go along with a deception that you would not tolerate if you had not become oppressed. You may have unknowingly abandoned your Kingdom or your expression in the moment. You may have listened to an opinion or a deceptive belief (the Impostor's undermining voice) in your thoughts without identifying or refuting. You may have allowed it to speak in your mind, without retrieving your moment. There are no triggers in the spirit's moment.

The spirit has a natural awareness in the moment and is able to stop and identify what is going on. There is a signal it gives you to warn you of danger. Learn it and obey it. That signal is different for everyone.

If you are suddenly feeling lowered, or you feel you are exhausted and losing power, or if you feel that you are on the brink of losing your divine consciousness, stop, identify, and resist! Connect with God. Take your moment, thoughts, and expression back with a consecrated determination. You are separate from deception and are no longer available to give it dominion over your life. Take your power back!

Mortify Via Holy Expression

"Impostor, I am not going unconscious. I am not unconscious now. I am not bowing to any trigger, to a familiar spirit, to any energy fluctuations, to the past or any deceptive thought. There is nothing wrong with me, except your belief that there is. I separate myself from you, by the reality of my redemption. Right here and now, I have authority over you."

Now, feel and hear what is going on in the moment. Hear what "fear" is saying and identify who you are not, including all the thoughts, words, feelings, and unconscious triggers that do not belong to you. As you do the talking and declare your truth, you are mortifying the Impostor's mentality. You are mortifying the deeds of the flesh.

"For if ye live after the flesh, ye shall die but if ye through the Spirit do mortify the deeds of the body, ye shall live."
—Rom. 8:13

If you feel yourself losing clarity, being numbed, getting body pain, becoming irritated or disempowered, stop the Impostor in its tracks, in the moment. If you are suddenly having anxiety, becoming hyper-sensitive or feeling less than who you are, begin to pray, identify, and speak against it, in the moment. Choose to feel the emotion it is using to take your Kingdom down. Do not allow yourself to be repressed. The Impostor might be overwhelming you with its rage or anger. Feel it a bit, become aware of the emotion it is using to take you down, then turn on it and let it know you are on to it! You will witness yourself coming back to life. You will be undoing its emotional dump. Resist. Mortify. This is the spirit not receiving oppression. If you do not receive the oppression, you will not be triggered. You never have to be triggered again. You are about to gain light years in Divine Consciousness. This is "you," the spirit guarding your heart, doing your job. This is your vessel job description—remember, you are the "Heart Keeper" of your temple.

Take Your Kingdom Back by Force

Do not allow the Impostor's words to enter into your heart. Do not watch them. Do not think about them. Do not ignore them. Do not agree with them. Do not consider them. Do not allow them to speak their way into your heart! Stop them with Godspeed:

> *"Hey, Impostor, not one more word—not one more. How dare you attempt to speak into my heart; how dare you intrude on my territory. Do you think I am going to allow you to speak into my heart, change my mood or my emotions, bring me down or lower my spirit? Do you believe you are going to create lying symptoms, inflammation, illness and pain in my temple? You are deluded and have no truth".*
>
> *I am complete in Him who is
> head over all rule and authority—*
> —Col.2:10

> *"You are not going to co-mingle with my Christ. This is not your temple. I have the mind of Christ—how dare you try to intervene with my destiny? I am outraged at your boldness. Who do you think you are? I know who I am. Let me remind you, you are a fake, a bluff, a counterfeit of me—an illusion, a carnal mesmerization. I am the real thing, an authentic child of God, the carrier of the Christos, the Righteousness of God in Christ. I am called with a Holy calling. I am alive with Christ."*
> —Eph.2:5

> *"You will not undermine my awareness or silence my sacred expression. I speak my truth in the moment. I do not agree with you or any of your words of doubt or judgment. I am not in your darkness or denial. I uphold my integrity in Christ. I do not go unconscious.*

*I do not get lulled into passivity or any going along
with your attempts to oppress me. I do not go down.
I do not bow to you. I do not bow to any generational
familiar spirit or principality."*

"I am far from oppression and will not live in fear."
—Isaiah 54:14

*"You do not repress my feelings in the moment
or oppress my consciousness. You do not take my
territory. I take yours! I am on to you."*

"I am free from the law of sin and death"
—Rom.8:24

You Manifested Yesterday

Your heart is a natural manifestor. Always a co-creator with God or with the flesh, your heart has been bringing to pass God's words or the Impostor's all along. Your heart is on automatic word production. You now have a choice, a new way to change what you are creating. You can arrest the creations of the Impostor's reign. You now have an option to agree with God. God is in this new moment. Choose this day what you will manifest.

"Choose this day who you will serve."
—Joshua 24:15

Just as your battle is in the moment, every new word is in the new moment; each word received in your mind, is opening or closing your heart. Take your power back in this moment right now. Take it back. The good news is that God has created your heart to have the capacity to go into the next new moment and to stay open, by your walking after the spirit.

Therefore, there is now no condemnation in Christ for those who walk not after the flesh, but after the spirit. Walk away from this lie to grace. Do not allow your heart to become bitter, angry, or fearful. When you feel these emotions in your heart, it is not your heart's natural state. Rather it is the thoughts or unconscious beliefs that you have recently received from the carnal mind, the mind of the Impostor. Trauma received, can be dissolved by breaking its energy in the action of the new moment...Keep moving!

Often in deliverance ministry (inner healing by separation), when I remove a "spirit of fear," for example, I am casting it out of the heart. It is not of the heart. However, if the heart has been oppressed by the thoughts of the carnal mind, its ability to function is constricted by fear. We often refer to this as being "shut down." In truth, your heart is being blocked by thoughts, feelings and beliefs previously received and allowed into your heart, by your agreeing with the Impostor's perceptions. These are not entities, devils, or little green men—these are not aliens from Mars! Your agreement with words becomes the condition of your heart. This can change immediately, as soon as you become aware of these conflicting thoughts and deny them.

I have noticed the backlog of the Impostor's thoughts usually takes about three days to clear. Your heart will automatically produce the fruits of the new words received. It will also produce from the old words no longer being received. Fewer words and less input are a joy to the heart. When you eliminate the babbling of deception, peace is restored. You will feel a deep breath of relaxation. No thought is good thought.

Surrender Mind Control

If you decide today to not receive thoughts that you have identified to be obsessive or all-consuming, and if you decide to lay the latest mental thought idol down, arresting its destructive pattern, your life will be changed by the end of the week. You will feel as if a heavy weight has been lifted; your heart will open, and your spirit will rise. You will also become a privileged recipient of the revelation on the very subject you may have been over-thinking.

As you arrest negative thoughts entering your heart, you will be unblocking your natural ability to hear truth.

When I find myself in a mind-jam, I lay everything down. I get out of my head and my house. This is surrender.

I wait on the Lord in an ambulatory state. I do errands, go to the mall, get my car washed,—it never fails. God will use His Universe to speak to me. I have agreed by faith to lay the mental idol of mind control down. I am moving ahead without thought.

The synchronicity of circumstances will begin to manifest. Every person I run into will repeat the same thing over and over. I have seen God change the behavior of friends. Suddenly, a person who is usually very calm will be babbling loudly or speaking dramatically at me. God is revealing what I am projecting, where I have gotten lost and may have submit

Your Holy Identity

my identity. Sometimes if I am really stuck, it may take a day or two, but very soon, I will see it, laugh, and be grateful for God's revelation. Once the generational trigger is acknowledged, I am empowered and transformed. That, in and of itself, will break the mind jam. Let go. God is always speaking to you. It doesn't have to be audibly or with thunder and lightning.

Proactive Spirituality

This is proactive "Christos-Sanity," agreeing with God as a partner, as a child of the Spirit, one with a supreme inheritance. The flesh is conditioned to wait for an attack, then to beg for a healing. You, the spirit person, can move ahead by faith and always call a battle. Remember, a battle you call is a battle you win. This is the cure for trauma, moving ahead and not receiving the beliefs of the old nature in the moment. Trauma no longer belongs to you. If it does, then you are not a spirit being. Call its bluff!

There is no denial in the spirit. You, the warrior of your Kingdom, know it is righteous to confront evil in the moment. You would never tolerate being pushed back by a "generational familiar spirit." Who you truly are has a plan, a proactive warfare plan, to guard your Kingdom and advance in territory—you rock by faith!

> *"Take therefore no thought for the morrow: for the morrow shall take thought for the things of itself."*
> —Matt. 6:25

Chapter 15
Righteousness Consciousness versus Sin Consciousness

What follows is a very powerful chapter. It has transformational and healing power. It has the capacity to heal the unconscious mind, to change your generational beliefs, and to raise your spirit to its rightful position.

A Prophetic Warning

If you feel an oppression while you are reading this chapter, or if you feel any resistance or suddenly become tired, just begin to feel your feelings and identify them. Do not allow the resistance of the old nature's self-exaltation to repress you with its emotion of rage.

Remember, the flesh is provoked when you are gaining power over it. Your receiving revelation, or gaining awareness or authority are its demise. Begin to trust and honor your innate discernment and continue reading. Remain in the moment and respond consciously to what is going on. Let the Impostor know you are going to continue reading and you have no intention of becoming passive or receptive to its manifestations.

You are radically alive and supernaturally awake as the spirit being. You will not be stopped!

As you make your decision to not be silenced, you can choose to stand up and read out-loud, to boldly push through any oppression! You can shout the material over the Impostor's unconscious thoughts. You do the oppressing! The feeling of being exhausted, needing to sleep, or being compromised into a stupor (a going down) is just the Impostor repressing feelings. It is not you!

The Impostor is battling you for your divine rights and position. It does not want you to move ahead or gain any insight into its antagonistic behaviors. A new revelation is about to be birthed within you! It may come as you read in the moment. It may come when you leave this material and begin to focus on your day. It may come tomorrow. Soon, you will suddenly feel the elevation of being in your Holy Identity.

Rightful Position

Taking your rightful position of being upheld, as the spirit person back, is enforcing your God-given grace. Your grace has been freely given and covers all your situations. All of them! You do not have to receive being shut down to your aliveness ever again. Refuse to be shut down. Refuse to suffer needlessly. Evil is calling your bluff. The Impostor wants you to believe that you can be tossed from the Kingdom of God, that your heart can be shut down to your grace, that your sanctification can be disallowed, terminated by an error on your part. It wants you to believe that if you make a mistake you are in the curse of the law, fallen from grace, disapproved of, rejected, and out of the will of God. The Impostor wants you to believe that you can be disconnected from your Kingdom within.

The Old Law

The Impostor is attacking you with Old Testament rules and laws. These laws do not apply to you. If these laws are relevant, then Christ did not die on the Cross and redeem you from the law. This is the old Law of Sin and Death. You are in the "Perfect Law of Liberty." You have been made new, now. New law, new game.

> *"A new heart also will I give you, and a new spirit will I put within you: and I will take away the stony heart out of your flesh, and I will give you a new heart of flesh."*
> —Ezekiel 38:2

Game on in Christ

You have been, and you are now, redeemed from Sin Consciousness, victimization, self-justification, guilt, and condemnation. You are now able to perceive how condemnation and Sin Consciousness support deception and death.

Who could survive this law?

> *"For that which I do I allow not: for what I would, that do I not; but what I hate, that do I. If then I do that which I would not, I consent unto the law that it is good. Now then it is no more I that do it, but sin that dwelleth in me.*

For I know that in me (that is, in my flesh,) dwelleth no good thing: for to will is present with me; but how to perform that which is good I find not.

For the good that I would I do not: but the evil which I would not, that I do.

Now if I do that I would not, it is no more I that do it, but sin that dwelleth in me.

I find then a law, that, when I would do good, evil is present with me.

For I delight in the law of God after the inward man:

But I see another law in my members, warring against the law of my mind, and bringing me into captivity to the law of sin which is in my members.

O wretched man that I am, who shall deliver me from the body of this death?

I thank God through Jesus Christ our Lord."
—Rom. 7:15—25

This is Paul describing his experience in the war between the flesh and the spirit. Notice, he is not allowing himself to become guilty for what he is tempted to do when he knows it is truly not him doing it! He is declaring, "It is not me, but it is sin that dwells in my members. Who should deliver me from the body of this death? I thank God for Jesus Christ our Lord."

The Entrance of Thy Word Bringeth Light

This law might not be in your current awareness. You have probably not been taught to guard your heart from it. You might unknowingly be indulging its dogma. This is an unholy attack on a very deep and dark unconscious level.

Before the Cross of Christ redeemed us from the old law (the law of sin and death) people were punished for every law broken. No man or woman could keep the law and no man or woman could escape it. Whether they believed in God or not, this religious law remained at the root of every religion. This is not just true for Christianity. It is religious law, neither Christ nor God. You have an opportunity, as a believer, to be redeemed from it.

> *"But now we are delivered from the law, that being dead wherein we were held; that we should serve in newness of spirit, and not in the oldness of the letter.*
>
> *For without the law sin was dead.*
>
> *For I was alive without the law once: but when the commandment came, sin revived, and I died."*
> —Rom. 7:6-9

We are delivered from the law! You are being delivered from thinking that that this law belongs to you. You are being delivered from feeling shameful, guilty, or sinful, when you err or are deceived. We become aware that we are in the school of the spirit learning how to stand in our holy Identity and know that when we are deceived into bowing to the flesh it is not

Your Holy Identity

who we are. It is literally not you! When you understand this, you become free and empowered to stand against its wiles. This is what you would do...when you are assured it is not you. It is not an error that you need to fix! You cannot receive the fullness of your grace if you feel it is you that compromises. You cannot receive grace from a guilty conscious or from a sin consciousness. The Impostor knows this. You are not in the fullness of your redemption if you are agreeing that you are wrong or if you believe that you are a guilty, dirty, condemned sinner with every imperfect move you make. This is the law in your members that is warring the law in your mind!

You cannot agree with this law if you do you sign for it, you have no stand, and you discount your true identity. The Impostor has deceived you into submitting your redemption to sin consciousness, which is the very opposite of your divine truth.

> *"So then, I myself in my mind am a*
> *slave to God's law, but in my sinful nature*
> *a slave to the law of sin."*
> —Rom. 7:7-25

You are not in the old law. You do not need to get caught up in the vain works of trying to fix yourself. This self is not your true identity. You are trying to fix that which is not fixable. You are not it. You are so much greater than what you may be seduced into attempting to fix. You are fixed! You are all that! There is an expression, "You are not all that." It is the opposite of your reality. In redemption, you truly are all that and more in the fullness of your Christos!

When you trying to persuade yourself to believe something that you already are, to receive something that you already have, you are not in your holy Identity, you are in the works of mental ascent. This is a wrong teaching. You are not in Christianity you are in the law of sin and death.

Too often the teaching of the current church proclaims that you are a sinner, that you are wrong, and that you must repent. However, if you have to repent for everything you do, you are not redeemed. In your holy identity, you stand against deception. Big difference! If you stand against deception, you are in the power of the spirit being. If you must constantly repent and be accused for every behavior of the old nature, you are identifying with being a carnal, mortal sinner. You are a victim with no stand. If you have no stand, you will be constantly tossed out of your Kingdom, and you will not live your redemption. The grace that "saves" you or "separates" you from who you are not is the power of the blood of Jesus. The word "saved" means separated from or sanctified from.

When you are sanctified, you are separated from your flesh and you stand against deception! You have the power to stand, because you know who you are, and that sin does not belong to you. The more sanctified you become, the more power you have to not receive the deceptions of the flesh, and the more you will be experiencing the fruits of the spirit, love, joy, peace, and power. All your spiritual gifts will be activated. This is the error that has been created by Sin Consciousness that the Lord is about to correct on Earth.

When this evil attack is brought under the subjection of the spirit, the vessels of God, will have miracle healing power to heal others and be who they are: Christ on Earth, in the fullness of their Christos.

What This Means to You Now

I am going to break this Word down into human behavior, how this affects you now, and how the human heart is suffering needlessly. This will help you grasp the reality of a "Radical Transformational Redemption," and how you can apply it on a daily basis to add quality and peace to your life.

To be led by the spirit is not to be under the law—this is a fact. Being led by God is to be on sacred ground, holy ground. It is a sanctuary from the law. When you are led, everything goes your way. There is a flow. The moment comes to you. You are in God's perfect will and purpose. It is truly all good.

However, on other occasions, you can be misled, and you might be deceived into moving in a wrong direction, one that does not feel good. You feel lowered, perhaps confused or triggered, and you may suddenly be losing mental clarity. These are warning signals to change your direction, as this may not be God's purpose.

We are all in the School of the Spirit here on Earth. This leading of the spirit is one of the things we are learning, one of our most important lessons. We have been given the ability to be led, which is a very natural God-given attribute, one that has already been perfected in your spirit. The Impostor battles us for our being led by the spirit, an innate divine right and a gift of grace. To be led by the spirit, the Impostor knows, is not to be under the law, no law in being led, no law in your spiritual fruits, no law in love, no law in the integrity of your moment. There is no law in your spiritual authority. It is divine wisdom to know holy ground, sacred ground, that the law cannot enter.

"To be led by the spirit is not to be under the law."
—Gal. 5:18

The Impostor's Guidance

The Impostor will always attempt to mislead you. It will mislead and confuse you with fear, doubt, and the re-stimulation of trauma. The Impostor uses fear triggers. It wants you to accept the judgement of the law! It is seeking an opening, an opportunity, a door in your mind to be ajar or unguarded. It seeks such an opportunity twenty-four hours a day, even in your sleep. The Impostor is always trying to gain territory. The Impostor wants to lead. Spirits of self-exaltation, doubt, condemnation, compromise, victimization, and self-justification want you to bow to their carnal perceptions and choices. The Impostor has thoughts, emotions, and a will of its own. Self-will, or "Counterfeit Consciousness," is always fear-based. The root is fear. It will use drama, creating a magnification of repressed emotions and a dumping of negative thoughts, creating more negative feelings. It will always justify itself.

The Impostor would like to indulge itself and distract you with emotional pain, pain that no longer belongs to you. It desires to utilize a trigger, one that may remind you of a familiar situation from your past, one where you have been disem-

Your Holy Identity

powered, abused, or victimized. This past no longer belongs to you, and neither does the trigger or trauma. You do not need to fix the situation that the familiar spirit has created. You need only to identify it and call it out in the moment.

This is God's "Holy Moment," a confrontation of the Impostor's fears, lies, and setups. This is where your divine rights and spiritual authority overcome the Impostor of your identity. This is where you stand against all intrusion by faith. This is where the spirit inherently reigns and the flesh bows to you. This is where all the teachings, all the ways to get to God, all the opinions and interpretations of man, interfere with your very grand inheritance. There is no higher ground than grace.

The Impostor knows this and fears that you will one day appropriate the only revelation that you need to have, to set you free from the Law of Sin and Death. After this timely revelation is imparted into your heart, you will understand that you can do it all wrong, move in a direction of error, bow to the flesh and all its works. This truth will be your end to a lifetime of unnecessary suffering. This is a "Radical Transformational Redemption," you may not have not been introduced to it till now. This is knowing who you are in your true essence and what Jesus did for you on the Cross. This is the end of condemnation and Sin Consciousness. This is where, the mercy of Christ, allows and encourages your education on the stage of glory, and the training of the Christos to empower your spirit. The Holy Spirit is instructing you about the your most important territory, the one that Christ left for you to conquer, to bring your flesh under subjection. This is the trial and error system of life; if you know who you are, you can go through this life in abundant gratitude and joy! God is not teaching you lessons via punishment or oppression. The Great "I am" is equipping you to walk in the fullness of your spiritual identity.

Once you see this as God sees this, how you and your spiritual journey are being perceived with a holy vision, you will be able to encounter the unconditional grace and mercy of Christ and joyfully accept each challenge as an opportunity to be promoted.

The following scripture is the revelation I am talking about. Many of you have never heard it mentioned before. You may doubt it is true. Go ahead, look it up. I will not be offended!

"The Spirit cannot sin!

Whosoever is born of God doth not commit sin;
for his seed remaineth in him: and he cannot sin,
because he is born of God."
—1 John 3:9

The Impostor tries to distract you away from the facts or your redemption and divine rights. It wants to blame you for its deceptions, sins, and errors. It wants you to blame the devil! The impostor wars you in your mind, in your members, hoping you will blame the devil, blame yourself, blame someone else, and then submit to a bow to Sin Consciousness. It fights your mind for your divine and unconditional grace and wants you to believe that the old law is still in effect. It knows many people are not aware of the fullness of their redemption. Many

Your Holy Identity

people still believe they are sinners. They brag about it and confess it all day long. The Impostor has been able to limit our belief and knowledge of our redemption for a long time.

The Impostor wants to disempower the mind of Christ and have it seen as a religious offering: an unconscious, religious, pious mind. However, the mind of Christ is the divine mind, with dominion on Earth. You, in your Holy Identity, are a partaker of all the fruits of the spirit. Often, the Impostor has been invited by ignorance to allow religion to oppose your natural conscious state, creating an oppressed consciousness. It may use accusations of your being wrong, misled, or angry, accuse you of having resentment and guilt, or suggest you are in error. It will use anything you will acquiesce to in order to keep you out of your Divine Mind and your true identity. Righteousness Consciousness is always your divine right.

The Impostor wants to set you up, blind you to its wiles, and have you led by self-will. Then it will blame you for being misled. It is a set-up to condemn you. The Impostor is aligned with religious law, Sin Consciousness. It is operating in its old law pre-Christ reality. This is Old Testament pre-Christ Law, The Law of Sin and Death, the very law that you have been redeemed from! Remember beloved, the blood of Jesus was shed on the cross to take your from the Law of Sin and Death to the Perfect law of Liberty! By one blood offering you were translated and transformed!

The Impostor wants you to believe that every time you are not on the exact mark, not perfectly led, every time you move in a less than perfect direction or make a less than perfect decision, that it has a legal right to punish you. It wants to trigger you and then shut you down in the old nature's laws, from victimization to condemnation. It wants you to feel guilty about your past and focus on it (the very past it created by controlling your life). It thinks it can create a fall from grace and shut down your heart and Kingdom power.

What's God Got to Do with It?

Sin Consciousness is not the path of Christ. This path of severe condemnation is unable to edify your spirit or your heart. There is no room for error, no mercy on its path, no grace to learn or grow. This is not Righteousness Consciousness. This is not the will of God. This is an attack on your divine rights, your incorruptible seed, and your redemption. If these deceptions are accepted as true, if you think you are still a lost soul, a sinner, the Cross of Calvary has been made null and void in your life. You are innocently seduced into disagreeing with the finished work of Christ.

This attack is prevalent in today's perceptions of Christianity and is present in all religions: Karma in Buddhism and Hinduism, purgatory in Catholicism—all religions have created "the payment." The Muslim religion is totally law-based. There is no mercy or forgiveness of error. There is a price to pay, a punishment for everything from mind to body and there is no spirit in it. Then, the Impostor blames God for this repercussion. The Impostor thrives on this lack of knowledge. Without this ability to attack a human heart with condemnation, guilt, and the "fear of" punishment, on this level of the old law, the

Impostor has no power. I want to make this point absolutely clear: this shutdown of your heart is not Christ. It is not conviction. It is the Impostor's works, to hold you back, to keep you down, confused, and most importantly, *not moving ahead.*

Stuck

The Impostor wants you entangled and busy, always recovering from its errors. It wants you bowing, blaming, sacrificing, and giving up your heart's desires. It wants you ill in doubt and condemnation, confused in works, feeling sick, depressed, and cancelling your life, every day—it wants you stuck. The Impostor wants you waiting to get it right, waiting passively to recover from some alleged lying symptom. It wants you immobilized and disabled.

Moving ahead has faith in it. Faith is your most powerful weapon against the Impostor. The Impostor ponders, worries, and introspects. "Impostor" territory is a focus on the old self. Spiritual territory is outside of your old self, out of the constant focusing on the old pre-redeemed you, out of the compulsive going within to seek counsel from who you are not.

The truth is, you are not physically ill, and you are not tired. You are oppressed or repressed from a deception that you have innocently received. You may have received the oppression of a trigger. You may have unknowingly and naively been deceived into bowing to the Impostor's perceptions and will. This is the Impostor keeping you from the truth of your sanctified position.

Your generational past victimizations will attempt to come up, to take back the territory you have taken from it. This is natural, a part of the war between the flesh and the spirit. This will happen often as you are learning to enforce who you are. God does not want you undermined, oppressed, or depressed, because you missed a mark or missed a moment.

It is not God's will or intent to teach you something by creating pain, anger, triggers, or doubt. There is no need to wonder what happened, what may have occurred to have shut you down, or what may have given you anxiety. It is not God's desire to have you suffering and in the dark about the causes and effects of events in your life. It is not God's will for you to have to call constantly for prayer, or believe you are under a constant attack of the Devil, or some other outside influence. The King of the Universe does not encourage the blaming of your parents, friends, past, spouse, or anyone else. The Spirit does not look back! These are not the ways of the Lord. This is not Christ, God or Christianity.

> *"Brethren, I count not myself to have apprehended: but this one thing I do, forgetting those things which are behind, and reaching forth unto those things which are ahead..."*
> —Phil. 3:13-14

A Hip Warrior

God wants you to be a "hip" warrior. God wants you to take the responsibility of apprehending the very next new moment and to move on to receive your grace and revelation.

You have been redeemed from spending your life in a perpetual recovery state of being. That is the flesh suffering from a life from which you have been translated. God wants you to take your grace back. This is a part of your redemption. You have already been given the power to do this, in your spirit, and you have the help of God's Holy Spirit the minute you step out in faith!

In the previous chapters, you were instructed on how to stop a trigger. You will now learn how to stop the "attack," even if you missed the moment and didn't stop, identify, or resist the trigger. You will be stopping all the triggers from the flesh very soon. You will be mortifying the deeds of the flesh as you practice being who you already are. You are going to learn how to arrest the being "punished" by the condemnation and fear of the Impostor when it is blaming you for its deliberate and intentional opposing behaviors.

This is another part of your vessel job description, as the "heart keeper" of your temple, and you will win this battle. You are predestined to win. This is the most important battle you can identify and conquer here on Earth.

However, even as you are learning to enforce your grace in your perfected and sanctified position, you are still, always, and right now, your Holy Identity. Righteousness Consciousness is available now today, a free loan from the Bank of Grace.

Chapter 16

There Is Therefore Now

You never have to suffer from missing a moment again. You are about to learn how to enforce your grace even if you have been beguiled into bowing your identity to the flesh, when you have been seduced by a familiar spirit and may have gone unconscious for a moment in the battle, when you have been misled to move in a wrong direction, and even when you are deceived into doing everything in total error.

Today, you will learn how to stand in the absolute fact that, "there is therefore now no condemnation in Christ." Hallelujah!

Today, you will learn how to appropriate your new revelation as a weapon in your identity warfare. With this absolute scriptural truth:

*"…there is therefore now, no condemnation in Christ -
For those who walk not after the flesh, but after the spirit.*

*For the law of the Spirit of life in Christ Jesus hath
made me free from the law of sin and death…*

*for what the law could not do, in that it was weak
through the flesh, God sending his own Son in the*

likeness of sinful flesh, and for sin, condemned sin in the flesh:

That the righteousness of the law might be fulfilled in us, who walk not after the flesh, but after the Spirit.

For they that are after the flesh do mind the things of the flesh; but they that are after the Spirit the things of the Spirit.

For to be carnally minded is death; but to be spiritually minded is life and peace.

Because the carnal mind is enmity against God: for it is not subject to the law of God, neither indeed can be.

So then they that are in the flesh cannot please God.

But ye are not in the flesh, but in the Spirit, if so be that the Spirit of God dwell in you.

Now if any man have not the Spirit of Christ, he is none of His.

And if Christ be in you, the body is dead because of sin; but the Spirit is life because of righteousness.

But if the Spirit of him that raised up Jesus from the dead dwell in you, he that raised up Christ from the dead shall also quicken your mortal bodies by His Spirit that dwelleth in you.

> *Therefore, brethren, we are debtors, not to the flesh, to live after the flesh.*
>
> *For if ye live after the flesh, ye shall die: but if ye through the Spirit do mortify the deeds of the body, ye shall live. For as many as are led by the Spirit of God, they are the sons of God.*
>
> *For ye have not received the spirit of bondage again to fear; but ye have received the Spirit of adoption, whereby we cry, Abba, Father.*
>
> *The Spirit itself beareth witness with our spirit, that we are the children of God."*
> —Rom. 8:1-16

Now, right here and now, the Holy Spirit is about to upgrade your entire belief system and bring it up to Christ and His "Radical Transformational Redemption."

I am going to give some examples of daily human experiences so that you may learn how to take authority over the flesh, using your Righteousness Consciousness to evoke your divine rights for victory. There is nothing in your life that is more important than understanding this.

Every time you err in any way, walk left when you should be heading right, move slow when it should be fast, or say no when you should say yes, this law condemns you. It does so anytime you agree with doubt or worry. In fact, with any disobedience of the old law (miss a Sunday at church, sleep late, say a negative word, make a mistake, think a negative thought, accept a trigger, anytime you fall short of absolute perfection in anyway, miss the mark, and even when you are innocently misled) this old law condemns you. It is absolutely "critical" of every move you make.

Pre-Christ Law

Hear me now. This is not church talk, but life talk. This law that constantly attacks corruptible seed abides in the old creature. It has taken up residence deep in the unconscious soul in its pre-redemptive, untransformed state. This law exists until you confront it. It is not true; it does not belong to you. It is a belief operating on a bluff, a bluff that you must identify and call.

The Spirit of Fear

You are learning to inhibit, annihilate, and dominate the spirit of fear. We are all called to guard spiritual justice. The Impostor has no legal right. It is a bluff. We call its bluff by identifying its voice and pushing it back. We push fear back by the demonstration of faith. The action of faith has the final authority in the spiritual realm. The spirit has the final authority in the mental, physical, and emotional realm, and all matter.

> "God has not given me a spirit of fear, but of love,
> power, and a sound mind."
> —2 Tim. 1:7

A Sound Mind

A sound mind is a peaceful mind, a divine mind, a mind of wisdom, the spirit mind. Any conflict, indecision, stress, or worry, is not your mind. It is the opposition trying to undermine your identity. As you simply acknowledge your awareness of its plan, you will be mortifying its intentions.

Pick up your spiritual sword and push all opposition down. Declare with a focused rebuttal in the moment, one directed at each intimidating thought, responding word to word, to its rhetoric, to its voice:

"When the eye is single the whole body is full of light."
—Matt. 6:22

"I am single-minded unto the Lord; I do not ponder thought. I am no longer entangled with the yoke of bondage."
—Gal. 5:1

No Doubt in Out

Then move on. There is no doubt in out. No doubt in disengaging and moving on, out of the thinking mind. If you do not go in (in other words, become introspective) or think with the "In-postor," or allow any of its opposing thoughts to enter your mind, its interference will pass quickly. If you choose to negate giving any attention to its lying physical symptoms, it will bow to your authority. It is a mere mortal bluff. It has no power over you, once you *pull the plug of thought.*

The action of moving ahead by faith is you, the new seed, the living word, in demonstration. This demonstration evokes the presence, power, and authority of God. You will have a supernatural encounter with "the Great I Am."

How the Impostor Uses Fear

Every time the Impostor triggers your memory bank and you do not deny its undermining suggestions, you have been seduced out of your Holy Identity. You are then subject to the "fear of" syndrome which is a generationally inherited (hand me down) spirit of Sin Consciousness and its condemning power to shut down your heart. When you receive these carnal suggestions without identifying them, the Impostor is keeping you in darkness and denial, and this creates an immediate disconnection from your essence by using the "fear of" trigger system. There is a fear in your heart of being abandoned by you the spirit person. There is a fear in your heart of losing its protection and thereby losing its guard! This is a spiritual attack, and you are being manipulated, disabled, and distracted from being the guarder of your heart. After the Impostor has successfully taken over your mind, your watch, and your focus, it will accuse and condemn you for the error it has created! That is, of course, the Impostor's intent and purpose.

> *"That if our hearts do not condemn us, we have confidence before God."*
> —1 John 3:21

Hidden Fears

These fears and beliefs are hidden deep in your unconsciousness soul. They are in the old creature where there resides an innate automatic fear response, to a "Sin Memory" trigger and its repercussions. This is not in your "New Creature" identity, where all things have been made new.

> *"Our old man is crucified with him*
> *that the body of sin might be destroyed."*
> —Rom. 6:6

These are beliefs in mortality and agreement with inherited doubt, worry, and condemnation which insists that you are to be blamed, accused, and made wrong. Claiming that you have erred and that you should therefore suffer. The Impostor infers, by the abandonment of your mental guard, that you are a mere unconscious, helpless, sinful mortal, that you are corruptible seed, under the curse of the old law.

These erroneous beliefs create a "fear of" the Impostor's triggers, and a hyper-vigilant awareness, a consciousness of fear, doubt, error, and sin. These are fears that you may not have acknowledged, fears deep within your heart, because you are not aware of them. Due to your lack of awareness of their existence, you are unable to take care of yourself when they attack your mind in the moment, by "keeping" your heart from their deceptions. You are condemned and compromised by the Impostors beliefs. This is not conviction; this is your heart receiving condemnation. Remember, if your "heart condemns you not you have confidence toward God." Many psychologists might suggest that this is a "fear of" abandonment. In a way it is, but in truth, it is much larger and more primal than that.

It is the "fear of" the abandonment of your spiritual authority over the flesh.

When a "fear of" belief is accepted and not replaced with truth, there is an open door to your mind. This is an unspoken invitation for the Impostor to impose all of its thoughts of doubt, guilt, anger, rage, victimization, shame, and blame on you with all of its evil ancestral fruit and ungodly perceptions.

> *"Watch and pray so that you will not fall into temptation. The spirit is willing, but the flesh is weak."*
> —Matt. 26:41

Roots of Doubt

These "fear of" triggers are an identity issue. They are rooted in doubt, in doubting who you truly are "identity doubt." If the Impostor cannot oppress you with a trigger or a deceptive belief from your past, you will remain in the innate authority of your Holy Identity.

There is in your soul, an unconscious mortal "fear of" the Impostor's ability to shut you down and thereby oppress your life force, by judging and condemning you without mercy. When the heart receives these beliefs, it is told by deception to condemn you by the words it receives. Remember, your heart is responding to words. This is not conviction, but rather the receiving of the condemnation that Christ has redeemed you from.

There is a "fear of" the words, behaviors, and abuses (familiar spirits) of your parents and their ancestral past. This "fear of" is in their mortal DNA seed: corruptible seed.

These fears are theirs. They do not belong to you in your Holy Identity. However, you are most aware and receptive to the fears, doubts, and victimizations that are most familiar to you.

This is also inclusive of the trauma and victimizations you may have unknowingly received: any integrity you have been deceived to relinquish, and any idols that you may have agreed to submit to, having been under the illusion of this carnal deception.

This is the root of triggers: the "fear of" the Impostor's ability to deceive and oppress you in identity doubt. If you know who you are, in your Holy Identity, you cannot be united with doubt. You will remain sanctified.

Fear of

This is not fear. It is a "fear of." This is the spiritual definition of fear itself. Without a belief in Sin Consciousness and condemnation, these fear triggers are powerless. They are powerless because you were redeemed from them.

> *"Therefore, if anyone is in Christ, the new creation has come: The old has gone, the new is here."*
> —2 Cor. 5:17

Your Holy Identity

How the Impostor Proliferates "Fear of"

You may believe that you have a fear of your neighbor, a fear of your boss, or a friend, etc. However, it is not the person you are afraid of. It is the unconscious trigger, in your trauma memory bank, that the person you are feeling a "fear of" represents to you. This could be a "fear of" the spirit of condemnation or a "fear of" the spirit of doubt, of fear of victimization, of self-exaltation, or of self-justification. These fears may remind you of a person who exhibited these familiar qualities (spirits) in your past, or familiar spirits. These are generational principalities and strongholds.

For instance, if your father was a worried man (always thinking, spent a lot of time pondering, a lot of time in his head, unable to connect to you, or his surroundings) you might be triggered by a spirit of doubt. If your mother was a very bossy or controlling woman (always giving commands, aggressive, and this often felt overbearing to you as a child) you might be triggered by a spirit of control. If you were treated aggressively by a neighbor, you might have a fear trigger for aggressive men or woman. If you have been hurt or rejected in your past, you might have a fear of re-victimization. If you experienced a car accident and you were injured, you might have a "fear of" memory of blue Nissans.

There might be a link in your trauma memory bank of men with beards—perhaps the driver of the car that was involved in your accident had a brown beard. If you were sexually abused or physically beaten in your childhood, or adulthood, these traumas have a long reach and can expand on an unconscious level to most of the population.

There is also a "fear of" people that you have not taken care of yourself with, in your adult life, when you have become passive by the influence of the Impostor and have not expressed your truth in the moment, or you may have not set a necessary boundary. The more you let everything go, fear magnifies itself, until you may become afraid to leave your house, to go to work, to get married, or to express yourself. The list goes on and on. This constant turmoil can create illness, perpetual disharmony, repressed anger, or rage, and can attempt to destroy a sound mind.

It creates a compromise of your integrity, a constant bow to fear, and an inability to take care of yourself. This can become what is psychologically diagnosed as mental illness. This can also become what is medically diagnosed as chronic illness and chronic pain.

When a "fear of" one of these spirits from your past grips your heart, with an unconscious re-stimulation of a past trauma memory, it can temporarily disable you, taking a piece of your life force. This "intimidation" received can siphon your spirit power right out of your heart; it oppresses, quenches, and represses your essence. If you do not have an unconscious "fear of" this happening, it cannot harm you. It has no power over you. *It only exists in your agreement with it.*

My Healing of Hypersensitivity

I will share with you how I was able to receive the revelation of "fear of." As a former psychologist, my beliefs of trauma and fears were often challenged and renewed by the Holy Spirit. After I had been healed of all my illnesses, my diseases, my viruses, and my allergies, I was elevated by grace to divine health. Yet there remained one exception, and it was a big one. I had one thing left. I knew I would be healed of it. I had absolute faith for it; I just didn't know when or how. I was waiting on the timing of the Lord. I still reacted violently to the energy of people. I could receive an energetic blow and be sick, or be stuck in an oppression, confusion, or pain for days. I truly believed this reaction had nothing to do with me. I will explain my healing of hypersensitivity the best that I can; it was an illuminating and unexpected serendipity.

Often when God speaks to me or gives me a revelation, he imparts an experience. This ensures there will be no wondering, pondering, or doubt. My spirit gets raised to become and live the new truth.

The Belief of Hypersensitivity

Many people believe they are hypersensitive to energy, to people, to vibrations, or even to electromagnetic fields. I know I did. It was the final symptom of disharmony in my body that I was healed of and the most resistant. There is an entire school of thought that this is a reality and much education and research is being provided to validate and study the symptoms in the body induced by energetic "fields." There are many groups now meeting to commiserate about their hypersensitivities, and there have even been several movies made to justify and explain the symptoms. Yet, there have been no healings or solutions from these theories.

God led me to go on an extended fast, and while my spirit was in a heightened position after the fast, He revealed the root of these sensitivities to me. I was not reacting to energy, or people; I was not getting a transference of other people's pain or problems when I prayed for them, or any other kind of transferring of spirits. I was reacting to my own fear triggers.

Holy Spirit Deliverance Training

There were times in my life, after I would do a healing service, that I would spend the entire next morning casting out all the alleged transferring spirits that I believed I had received. I would spend hours a day in self-ministry. The Lord let it go for a while, as there was a purpose to it. He was teaching me my deliverance ministry, and I learned a lot. I was learning to bring deliverance up to a higher consciousness, to the "mind of Christ."

I was learning about fear and how it could be cast out of the mind and heart by the power of the Holy Spirit. I was learning that everything not of God has its roots in fear, that there was always a fear first before the naming of every spirit. For example, if I would cast out a spirit of victimization (a trigger of victimization), I would cast it out as a "fear of" victimization and the removal of this deception would be accelerated when it was properly identified.

My training in deliverance ministry was a wonderful and empowering time. Every day, for two years, God would instruct me on how thoughts and fears could shut us down, create illness, disharmony, and pain. He was teaching me the root of these spirits, and how to make a connection with the power of God to spirit, mind, heart, and body healing. I was learning that everything starts in the spirit, if the spirit is empowered, and in its purpose, and God-given Holy Identity, the body, mind, heart will naturally follow.

The individual purpose of the human spirit has tremendous power. When the deliverance teaching season was over, I was led to do a fast. I fasted for ten days. I had done a lot of fasting previously, and it was always different. I had no idea what was going to happen, and often I would get a revelation. That was my hope. But this time it was different. When this fast was over... Well, I will never forget the experience...

Becoming the Revelation

I was driving on the 101 Freeway in LA, I had just come off my ten-day water fast, and I had just met my best friend for a celebratory feast-after-fast lunch. She had been fasting also. We had just shared a huge Mexican meal at the Acapulco Restaurant on Sunset Boulevard in Eagle Rock, California. All of a sudden, on the drive home, I started to feel pain in my stomach area, a very intense pain. Immediately, the Impostor attempted its "throw me off the track," rationale: *"You ate too much. One does not go off a fast on heavy Mexican food. That was foolish."* That made sense to me for a moment, as people go off a ten-day fast on juice, cereal, something that is easy to digest. What was I thinking? The pain began to worsen. As a matter of fact, it got so bad I had to pull off the freeway and park my car on a side street. I was no longer able to drive. I was then sitting in my car, unable to move. The pain had all my attention. I began to pray, in an effort to separate myself from the pain, and to try to identify what was happening. I was led to handle it as the spiritual issue that it was. The large post-fast meal had nothing to do with my current pain.

I began to feel an intensity in the pain. As it was reaching a peak, it was unbearable. I began to wonder if I was under a demonic attack. The Impostor chimed in, when its devil blame attempt failed it went for the physical body, *"You have injured your stomach; you were crazy to have fasted for ten days without food, just water. You have created a serious problem, maybe even an ulcer."* At that point, the pain in my stomach began to move as if it were alive. The pain began to rise up, to crawl up my body. It was very fast and very strong. I had no time to ponder or take any control—I became the observer of some kind of a physical breakthrough...

It felt like a baby kicking, but larger, more powerful; the pain moved from my stomach to my mid-section to my chest. Then it moved from my chest to my neck, then my face, and finally released itself by going up and out through my head, and then it stopped. The pain ceased with the release. The spirit had accomplished what it had set out to do.

I sat alone in my car on a small side street, stunned. I suddenly realized I was in the fullness of my human spirit, higher than I had ever been before. My perceptions had been automatically changed. I was sitting in heavenly places with Christ Jesus. After a while, I began to comprehend and discern what had just happened. I had been privileged to be an overseer of the actual physical war of the flesh and the spirit. My spirit had pushed itself up against and over the block of the flesh and the spirit was now reigning. I had become me, in my Holy Identity. The flesh had been blocking my revelation, one that God wanted to impart to me.

I felt a strong desire to go to places and see people that I had previously been hypersensitive to. I was led to take some territory away from the Impostor. I went expectantly by faith to have a super-natural spiritual adventure with Christ.

I went to a lot of unusual places that day, places that I had deliberately avoided for years. I did not have a reaction to anything or anyone. I remember there was a non-Christian spiritual bookstore on Santa Monica Boulevard in Hollywood. In the past, I had to cross the street whenever I would walk past it, to quickly avoid it, and then I would actually turn my head away and look at something else. This store's very existence had always intimated me, causing me to receive a terrible headache.

I was led to walk into the store where I connected with and talked to the people that were employed there and I had no reactions. I picked up some of the books, and I read a bit just to show the Impostor I could, if I chose to. Still, I had no reaction. God revealed to me, as I was asserting my authority over the Impostor, that there was nothing wrong with anyone there, or anywhere else. The books were print, and they had no power over me. He shared with me that I had bowed to this deception, the deception of condemnation, and that He was the only power in the Universe. My physical reaction was coming from my personal bow, and the belief about it. The bow was disempowering me and making me rawly receptive to the illusions and intents of the carnal mind. This evil influence would attempt to separate me from humanity, using fear to keep me from the love and compassion of God.

That day, I went everywhere my carnal mind had insisted for years that I stay away from. I visited every local forbidden territory, negating with my new awareness the deceptive suggestions that certain people were possessed or that they had strong negative spirits, ones that could influence my well-being. The Impostor was ranting and claiming all day that I would get a "transferring spirit" or body pain. The Impostor's storytelling included the narrative that I was also sensitive to everyone else's thoughts and feelings. If someone was having a bad day, or a severe problem, I could not only feel it, but also become a part of it, being empathic to the energies themselves. God revealed to me that these were all beliefs of error, magnified fears and total lies, illusions. It was an amazing day of victory and freedom.

However, it did not end there. No, it went on and on. The Lord wanted me to be certain that the deceptions were exposed, encountered, and perceived for exactly what they were: a "fear of" trigger. The fear was coming from me, from my own deeply unconscious traumas, idols, and fears. I was not seeing the people as they were, but through my own carnally filtered, fear-filled interpretations, from the Impostor's mind, beliefs, and its illusionary projections.

This magnified awareness went on for thirty days. Every day, for thirty days, everywhere I went, I would feel the "fear of" mentality attack me. I would watch it. It always had the same intent: for me to believe that the problem was out there...

them. It wanted me to believe the problem was not mine. If I believed it was not my issue, I could not grow, I could not be healed. I would be living in agreement with the flesh, shut down towards much of life, living small, constricted, and in a state of projection, blaming others, blaming energies, blaming spirits, blaming the body, blaming devils, blaming instead of dealing with my own issues. A lifetime of bowing to self-justification! I would be stuck, not moving ahead, living in deception and doubt.

My gift as an empath, a gift of discernment, was given to be a divine gift, a blessing, not a condemnation!

If I agreed with the Impostor's beliefs, it could continue to shut my heart down, condemn me mercilessly, and create lying symptoms in my body, validating itself and all of its erroneous and insane generational beliefs.

The Impostor was using my carnal memory bank, the carnal "fear of" system, which is enmity against God and is in opposition to all humanity, to trigger me. God was illuminating me on the "mortal human condition." He was allowing me to understand the victimization of the human being, without the power of God, to separate itself from the evil within. I was in the process of a "Radical Transformation Redemption" healing.

Had I not had this experience for thirty days, I would not be able to know with absolute certainty that I had power over the "fear of" system and to know that you, too, have power over it. I was instructed on a daily basis on how to perceive it correctly, how to take authority over it, and how to be free of it forever. I was enlightened daily on exactly what it is.

As I lived it for thirty days, I watched it attack me, beguile me, and try to twist my thinking. Finally, after seeing it consistently for thirty days, I lost all my agreement with "fear of." I was then able to overcome it and bring it under subjection. It changed my life. I would observe my body tense up, creating neck pain, shoulder pain, headaches, nausea, back pain, inflamed tendons, and anxiety. My heart would shut down, be gripped in a "fear of" attack. Then, I would be led to take back my mind, retrieve the fullness of my identity and my Holy expression, and let the Impostor know it was a liar, a psychopath, and that I would not allow its deceptive thoughts, to permeate my consciousness. Never again would I be deceived by this error. I am incorruptible spirit, not mortal flesh, and I am redeemed from its laws and its ways.

Sometimes God saves the best for last. The healing of the alleged hypersensitivities to people, energy, electromagnetic forces, spirits, and all things outside myself was completed. I had given it a lot of power over the years. There were years I had allowed this erroneous belief to push me so far back that I could not even leave my home without getting reactions. I was forced to live fearing people and their energy. I had spent years reacting to something that didn't even exist; it was a very humbling revelation. I can only share the heartbreak of having relinquished many wonderful friends and relationships to this deception. I can humbly confess to the love lost and pain received for nothing, a total lie. I would never have guessed, figured it out, or learned of its hold on me by studying psychology. I would have never known that it was simply "fear of."

God is always revealing to us the next thing we need to see, the next level of truth we can receive at its appointed time. Once the Lord reveals something to us, it is our time to take it on, to walk it out by faith and overcome it, trusting that God has revealed it and He will be the fourth man in the refining fire.

This is the process of God—for us to go from glory to glory, from revelation to faith in action. What I had experienced in my body was the literal changing of the guard from flesh to spirit in my own temple, the war between the flesh and the spirit.

Beloved, you are in the Perfect Law of Liberty. You are sanctified form the Law of Sin and death.

All illness is from the curse of the law and you have been transformed, translated and redeemed from it by the Blood of Jesus.

All you need to do is know who you are, know who He is and know your divine rights stand against it. Amen!

Denial Is Not Transformation

If you have an unconscious fear of something that you erroneously believe is something that it is not, you can still be triggered. Denial is not transformation. If you have not confronted this evil with a righteous rebuttal, with scriptural fact, and separated yourself from it, aware of what it is, stopping its attempt to oppress you in the very moment of its mental attack, you are receiving its oppressive warfare without defending yourself. At the deepest root of every perceived human dilemma is this darkness, a "fear of" becoming powerless, compromised, and separated from our Holy Identity.

Growing in Authority

The good news is now that you know who you are in Christ, in your Holy Identity, you never again have to submit to a system that works against you. As you are growing in your authority and awareness to arrest the old creature and it's triggers, and to separate yourself from them, you may still live as the spirit person that you already are by grace. You will begin to take a detached position in your spiritual identity and not receive what no longer belongs to you. Detached, sanctified, these words have the same meaning—you can stand separated, flesh from spirit, and take authority over your fear with spiritual power. This is a "Radical transformation Redemption," a being saved (separated) in the moment.

> *"For the word of God is quick, and powerful, and sharper than any two-edged sword, piercing even to the dividing asunder of soul and spirit, and of the joints and marrow, and is a discerner of the thoughts and intents of the heart."*
> —Heb. 4:12

Generational Lifetimes of Compromise

The old creature is full of fear and triggers—that is its unholy consciousness. It has spent "generational" lifetimes adding idols, bowing to fear and doubt, and compromising. That is its nature. Many want to call this a sinful nature, which is a limiting interpretation. The "old creature" has a compromising nature, it is an idolater. I think that is a more accurate assessment.

The rest goes with the territory of relinquishing your essence. A sinful nature implies the flesh, points to the body, lusts, fornications, etc., focusing on material man. It is truly a spiritual issue, an identity dilemma.

The key is that you become aware of it and can identify, detach, and separate yourself from it by understanding it is not you. You are not mortal matter; you are a spirit being, you are God's beloved child, you are the divine seed of a living impeccable Christ. You are in fact "incorruptible seed" and spirit, the image and likeness of God. You are the very opposite of "corruptible seed" and all its compromises, illusions, and idolatries.

The Fear of Our Separation from God

In every human heart and soul, there is a fear of our identity being subverted and our predestined purposes and connection to God being denied. A life misinterpreted and, spiritually speaking, not lived. This misinterpretation creates depression, grief, and deep sadness. We are often, at that moment of despair, further deceived with a psychological self-justification, a distracting suggestion that we are feeling dissatisfied due to a relationship, a wrong diet, a hormonal imbalance, an illness, a childhood dilemma, a financial difficulty, etc. All these deceptions are very carnal and undermining interpretations of our supreme reality and divinity. The flesh is always blocking us from making the connection of identifying the root of illness and disharmony with spiritual vision.

> *"The first man is of the Earth, Earthy. The second man is the Lord from Heaven."*
> —1 Cor. 15:47

Radical Redemption

You have options, my friends. You can spend years in therapy discussing your past, trying to work it out, trying to fix your mortal old creature victimized self. You can become aware of every behavior and every trigger that you may have received from your parents, and their parents, all the way back to the beginning of time—or you can receive and be grateful for the grace of God.

Personally, I like to break the battle down to a legal issue. *"Impostor, I separate myself from you by the blood of Jesus. You have no legal right to undermine my Holy Identity. You are in the Law of Sin and Death and I am in The Perfect Law of Liberty. I am on to you, I know who I am, I know who you are, I know who my Heavenly Father is, and I know my divine rights, my authority, and the laws of the Spirit. There is therefore no condemnation in Christ. I know who has delivered me from the body of this death by grace...You have no legal right and no reality...I stand here and now in the next new moment of God! The grace of God. I am spirit and the spirit cannot sin."*

This is a rapid bottom-line stand and it has power to resolve all doubt and bring the Impostor under subjection.

Once the Impostor realizes you know who you are, it is deflated, and you will feel fear bow to you. You might even feel it responding with anger or rage. Be very aware that this is not you—it is the emotion of the Impostor losing a battle, and it is a sore, immature, overconfident loser. The flesh dies hard. Give it no place.

> *"I am crucified with Christ: nevertheless I live; yet not I, but Christ liveth in me: and the life which I now live in the flesh I live by the faith of the Son of God, who loved me, and gave himself for me."*
> —Gal. 2:20

Chapter 17
Christos-Sanity

Walking after the Spirit

The key to upholding our identity is walking in the spirit—actually, walking after the spirit, following the spirit. Sometimes, this even manifests as being redirected with the spirit in the lead.

Remember, "There is therefore now no condemnation in Christ for those who walk not after the flesh, but after the spirit." Let's go back to our lives: a real day. You wake up and you may not be feeling a flow in the spirit. You feel tired. Perhaps you have a headache. Your mind begins to ponder what happened. The Impostor suggests the flu, a cold, a sore throat, anxiety, depression, etc.

We have established what really happened in the previous chapters. You missed a moment or perhaps you were influenced by a trigger, no more and no less. Having your awareness raised to this spiritual reality can save you hours of being used, abused, and further shut down. You could be attempting to discover what the real problem is while the Impostor is busy manipulating you to calling your friends, calling doctors, and researching your symptoms on the Internet. The Impostor is willfully keeping you in its mentality: feeding your heart with its words, manifesting as it thinks and speaks. If you are able to conclude and discern that you were simply triggered and misled, and subsequently went into denial, innocently forgetting to default to your spiritual fruits in your "Holy Identity" you will see it for what it is: A trap! You were temporarily entangled in the passive, oppressive trance of error, and then...

You Begin to Remember Who You Are

You are your Holy Identity and you were deceived into giving your moment up; you bowed your moment. Now all you need to concern yourself with is taking it back and taking it back as fast as possible. That is the answer to all the Impostor's stealing of your time, attempting to manifest its words and speak them into your heart.

The Impostor may be busy creating a carnal "mind spin," a setup of evil, to have you pondering, wondering, and questioning, all leading to doubt personified. Your goal now is to return to your Holy Identity.

Your only desire now is to walk after the spirit. There you know that a clear mind awaits; there you will feel good and be led once more. It is there that the revelation you want exists and is abiding in clarity. Walk fast by faith, taking no thought. Do not allow the carnal mind to speak into your heart.

> *"Who by taking thought can*
> *add one cubit to his stature?"*
> —Matt. 6:27

Grace is the next new moment of God. Do the next thing—take a new action. The key now is to take no carnal thought, no thought at all. Moving on without thought is the portal to the new moment. You are walking after the spirit, and you will be risen by faith.

Divorce yourself from all thinking. Do not allow the Impostor to break your flow, your continuity, your apprehending your moment by thinking in its carnal thought process. The new moment is sacred ground in which there is no law. There is no old law in "surrender." Go forth by faith with a desire in your heart to reconnect, understanding that the emotion of love, when you are connecting with another human being, has the power to open *your* heart. You are love, and there is no law in love.

"Whoever lives in love lives in God, and God in him."
—1 John 4:16

The laws of Sin Consciousness reside in the carnal mind. Let go of all thought and walk into the next new moment. Know what you are doing and choose it; do not allow the Impostor's mind to look back. *"No Impostor, I am on to you; I am going to open my heart by faith. I am letting go of everything, I am going to connect with my fellow humans. When I connect, Impostor, it is in divine love. Love is who I am."*

There are no triggers in divine love. None! Choose to walk into the "reconnection" by faith in who you are and your faith in your divine love.

> *"There is no fear in love. But perfect love drives out fear, because fear has to do with punishment"*
> —1 John 4:8

The Spirit Is Life

The spirit is life. There are no old sin and death laws in life. There is no law for those who walk not after the flesh, but after the spirit. Stand now on this word. God is about to manifest.

There is no law in the next new moment walking after the spirit, no law in grace, no law of sin and death, in the fruits of the spirit. When there is no old law controlling your mind, there is no attack, no law, no trigger. In sum, no old law means no "Sin Consciousness."

There is no old law in walking in the spirit and no law in walking after the spirit by faith. There are no Sin Consciousness laws in your faith. The Impostor cannot come into your new moment; it is sacred ground. Do not be deceived into battling the Impostor for your situation or circumstance or in trying to find out what happened. Don't look back. Fight for your moment.

> *"Forgetting those things which are behind, and reaching forth unto those things which are before, I press toward the mark for the prize of the high calling of God in Christ Jesus."*
> — Phill. 3:13-14

Know the spiritual laws in the Universe in which you reside and negate the laws of Sin Consciousness with your divine rights and the fruits of your redemption...

"But the fruit of the Spirit is love, joy, peace, forbearance, kindness, goodness, faithfulness, gentleness and self-control. Against such things there is no law."
—Gal. 5:22–23

Life in the Spirit

Staying, or remaining in the spirit, is our ultimate goal, being always able to be who we are in our Holy Identity. God's grace has a plan for this. It is a conscious, easy-to-do, organic plan. God would not give you an impossible task. God is on your side, the side of the spirit.

This is your organic Jesus: the Christ in you, your Christos in Christos-Sanity. It represents dominion over your body, heart, and mind. Righteousness Consciousness is not shared with the man-made Christianity of religion.

There are many ways to conquer the Law of Sin and Death and also mortify the deeds of the flesh. A simultaneous dying to the flesh and rising up in the spirit is an on-the-job, ongoing, joyful, and a warrior-empowering training experience. Hallelujah!

Exposing Sin Consciousness

It will behoove you to continue to expose Sin Consciousness in your own precious heart, then in the hearts of others, one beautiful heart at a time. Today, it is being exposed in your precious heart. Tomorrow, you may desire to share your awareness with love and renew another soul to Righteousness Consciousness. It is a higher energy, a divine vibration; it is contagious. Just as negativity has a mental alignment with evil, Righteousness Consciousness has within itself the power and love of God.

The Attack of Guilt and Condemnation

The deception of guilt and condemnation is beginning to be confronted and rebutted on the Earth at this time. This is the opposing belief that has attached itself to religious Christianity. This is the Christos inhibiting belief that many good people have not identified and thereby have forfeited their grace, joy, authority, health, and peace. You cannot fall from grace; you cannot become the flesh. Just as a rose is a rose and a tomato is a tomato, a spirit is a spirit; it is a seed issue. Rethink redemption and stand on your divine seed and your position in "The Perfect Law of Liberty."

"In Him we have redemption-through His blood.
The forgiveness of our sins, according to
the riches of His grace."
—Eph. 1:7

God-Given Authority

The Perfect Law of Liberty has absolute dominion over the law of sin and death. "Righteousness Consciousness" reigns over "Sin Consciousness," and fear must bow to your God-given authority.

We must enforce the authority of our spiritual position. We must refuse to buy this anti-Christ scam, an evil belief that would make the Cross of Calvary powerless in your life.

You may freely live in the spirit—in the fullness of the fruits of the spirit. It is not possible for the flesh (mortality) to shut down eternal life or spirit. That belief is a mere fabrication, a carnal illusion of the law of sin and death itself.

Put the Impostor on notice. Renew your unconscious mind to The Perfect Law of Liberty and walk toward your destiny.

"Hey, Impostor: I am crucified with Christ. Therefore, I live, alive, my heart open and feeling deeply with great love and compassion for mankind. I am free in The Perfect Law of Liberty, a radically alive, resurrected, sanctified, and holy irrepressible spirit."

"My life is dead, I am hid in Him."
—Col. 3:1–4

"I am abiding in Him—grafted into the vine."
—Rom. 11:17

> "I am walking in His love and peace, three feet behind Jesus. *You, Impostor, are a fake, a bully, and a counterfeit. You have no life. You have no authority.*"

> *"Inherit the Kingdom of God prepared for you from the foundation of the world."*
> —Matt. 25:34

If you are willing to comprehend the incredible power of your God-given position, your life has just been changed and you have received your transformation from Sin Consciousness to a "Radical Transformational Redemption." Your Christos is reigning. You are in Christos-Sanity.

Chapter 18

Laying the Idols Down

You are not following man. You are following God. You will get what you came to get here on Earth, more power, more love, more spirit, more of God.

We have established that you are here to win this battle and gain territory. You are here to overcome the flesh, the Impostor of your identity.

You have learned in the previous chapters how to disentangle yourself from the Impostor thinking in your mind by arresting its thoughts. You are now in the process of identifying its input and able to rebuke error and retrieve your mind from deception.

A Conscious Surrender

This is surrender, an aggressive empowered agreement with God to abide in your Holy Identity.

Surrender is an action of faith. It can be defined as a walking away from the carnal mind, the "Impostor's thoughts" (all of them), and here comes the big secret: walking away from your carnal mind and everybody else's carnal mind. Take a proactive "I am here to win" spiritual attitude.

Do not become passive and submissive. Do not surrender to the wrong side. Do not surrender to religion. Do not surrender to people. Do not surrender to mind control. When you feel your mind is attempting to take over, or that your spirit is being oppressed by your intellect, take your spiritual characteristics back. Dwell in your spiritual fruits, in which there is no law. When you know who you are, you can deal real. You are not God's slave, but His beloved child.

Separate yourself from the Impostor's Sin Consciousness interpretations of your very grand inheritance, your spiritual truth and reality. A mind is a mind, and a spirit is a spirit. A spirit knows and has the answer that the Impostor is perpetually seeking.

> *"But God has revealed it to us by the Spirit.*
>
> *The Spirit searches all things, even the deep things of God.*
>
> *For who among men knows the thoughts of man except his own spirit within him?*
>
> *So too, no one knows the thoughts of God except the spirit of God.*
>
> *We have not received the spirit of the world, but the Spirit who is from God, that we may understand what God has freely given us."*
> —1 Cor. 2:11

The Impostor's counterfeit mind beckons you to think yourself into a solution, thereby creating the very block that is preventing your truth from being naturally revealed. It does the unnatural thing—it ponders.

Identifying the Mind of Fear

Thinking, thinking, thinking, in doubt, in confusion, and in fear. Wondering, questioning, engaging, and agreeing with worry. These are the fruits of the carnal ego mind, creating more deceptive thought, empowering and enlarging fear.

This is usually followed by the Impostor asking for help outside of your knowing, outside of God's lead and into the ways of man.

> *"But the natural man does not receive the things of the Spirit of God, for they are foolishness to him; nor can he know them, because they are spiritually discerned. For who has known the mind of the Lord that he may instruct Him? But we have the Mind of Christ."*
> —1 Cor. 2:14–16

Remember, you already know what the Impostor is seeking. You can forego hours of pondering—yes, days of introspection. Come on now, you know it is true. Sleepless nights, days of anxiety, worry and wondering. Years wasted in deep thought without action, being stuck in doubt. Fear and worry hold back your move of faith and enlarge deception by creating with each thought a submission to the ego mind of the flesh. Do not condemn yourself for this very human activity—it is just the old law in Sin Consciousness. It is the Impostor of your identity exploiting your innocence.

> *"But the anointing which you have received of him stays in you, and you need not that any man teach you: but as the same anointing teaches you of all things, and is truth, and is no lie, and even as it has taught you, you shall abide in him."*
> —1 John 2:27

A Spirit Doesn't Ponder

When you know that you know, you take action. Yes, knowing leads to action. You are not trying to convince yourself by procrastinating, affirming, or planning. This is all doubt personified. A spirit bypasses all the worrying. An enlightened Spirit is not distracted by the thoughts of the Impostor.

A Spirit Takes Action

A spirit lives in the adventure of life and moves ahead by faith, trusting God and trusting itself. Your spirit has a oneness with God, an abiding with God's Spirit, and a confidence in the Christos within.

Your spirit is here to feel deeply, to grow and experience life, and to have an experience outside of the carnal mind. A spirit wants to love, to create, to connect and express itself authentically, and to share its gifts and light.

The spirit of God is always available to assist you in appropriating your heart's desires. This defies the stumbling block, the idols of the intellect. The spirit's life force identifies and inhibits the plot of self-exaltation, always wanting to create more teachings, the getting there by "the intellectual works."

> *"Ever learning, and never able to come to the knowledge of the truth."*
> —2 Tim. 3:7

The stumbling block of works, the plotting, the begging, the over-thinking works, the flesh praying with an agenda, the ritualistic works, the "old self" aggressively pressuring you into the stress of self-will and self-justification, pushing against and above your spirit being loud, fake, and obtrusive, attempting to lead you into false reality's "mind spins."

> *"Not because God willed that they should be rejected, not because of any fornication, but because of their unbelief in Christ. Because [they sought it] not by faith. Sought not the righteousness that comes from faith in Christ, but as by works of law; for they did stumble at the stumbling stone."*
> —Rom. 9:32

Your heart hates this, recoils at this spiritual ignorance and abuse. This is your heart's greatest fear, to be repressed in mind control. To be oppressed by self-exaltation and doubt. To be overcome by unconsciousness. To be rendered passionless in works.

> *"Who has saved us and called us with a Holy calling, not according to our works, but according to His own purpose and grace."*
> —2 Tim. 1:19

The Mind Jam

Actually, the mind of the Spirit is above thought. It is not busy thinking; it is busy being. Sin Consciousness wants to use your mind and corrupt your thoughts to bring you to the ultimate denial of your power in Christ.

Sin Consciousness is wrong identification personified. This unholy consciousness will use all the things of the world to influence you to decide to heal it, acknowledge it, and focus on it. It will attempt to persuade you to buy into its plan, to fix it as if it were you. It is always desiring to seduce you into total denial of your true self and the power of your God-given grace.

One powerful way to separate yourself from the Impostor is by your telling it who you are and what you are doing:

> *"Hey, Impostor, I am led by the spirit and not under the law. I am in The Perfect Law of Liberty. You do not distract me from my reality. You do not distract me from my territory. You do not distract me from my purpose."*

Any mind jam interruptions, by even the smallest rebuttal to its temptations, will give you more of your own spirit. Any time spent questioning is the evil Sin Consciousness itself, in which there is much old law. Let go and take control simultaneously.

Denial of Your Identity

Denial in and of itself is a spiritual warfare against you, it is Sin Consciousness denying your true identity. Sin Consciousness uses denial to tell you that you are not who you are. It will deny your very identity, your essence. It will attempt to undermine the fact that you are a spirit, the image and likeness of God—that is the spiritual definition of denial. A victorious life is in the separation from the old to the new—a life lived without denying who you truly are.

No Denial in Opposing Error

You are not in denial when you oppose a negative feeling with your spiritual authority; you can feel these emotions and simultaneously tell deception who you are. You are in denial when you are deceived into thinking it belongs to you. You spend your days feeling it, thinking about the why and how come of it, discussing it with anyone who will commiserate, and reliving it as if it is you. The practice of reliving error is re-victimizing yourself. This revelation can bring a life-changing difference.

Emotional Dumps

The old nature wants you to be at the mercy of its emotional dumps, or it may tell you that you are in denial by not feeling your feelings. Often these are not even your feelings, but the Impostor's own creations from its thoughts and behaviors. This is one of its greatest psychological deceptions. As a former psychologist, I needed some extra "Holy" counseling from the Lord Himself to recognize the depth of this deception.

The Impostor is as a subtle serpent. It can take a positive tool and turn it into another idol, a God unto its own, or suggest some "new way." There is no way but faith. The faith that is already in your heart and spirit, your innate faith is without mind control or works.

The Last Word

It is spiritually edifying to feel a feeling and tell the Impostor who you are simultaneously. The truth spoken over your heart interrupts the repression of feeling. It has the power to re-open your heart. The last word stands. Let it be yours.

The Impostor wants you in its mind jam of processing its new drama dump every day in "works" and staying there, getting stuck, examining its perceptions, feeling its feelings. It wants you entangled with emotions that are created by its thoughts and its unconscious fears and triggers. It wants you stuck, not letting go and becoming so overwhelmed and oppressed in the Impostor's "daily download" of negative thoughts and feelings and so confused that you are temporarily unable to connect to your own God-given authority. This is another way it makes itself an idol, one of its most reliable schemes. It wants you to lose yourself, your truth and separation, in its overwhelming doubt and constant conflicts.

> *"Stand fast therefore in the liberty wherewith*
> *Christ hath made us free and be not entangled*
> *again with the yoke of bondage."*
> —Galatians 5:1

Many a good heart have been oppressed in this mind jam and have had years of purpose and joy denied. This creates a sense of despair from being compromised and misled. This can be immediately and naturally healed, and your heart restored the very moment this mind jam is acknowledged, identified, and arrested. As soon as you arrest its lies with the demonstration of the next new moment being apprehended, as soon as you walk away from the Impostor, without thought, you are negating its sad tale. It will always have a rational story, and this interpretation of your reality is as far from the truth as the East is from the West.

Walking out of your old self (and all your alleged problems) into an authentic connection will re-open your heart. A connection has the power to break the mind jam of fear. Perfect love casts it out. Perfect love is simply you connecting with another human being. You are the carrier of the Christos.

Pondering Manifests Fear

The Impostor uses fear thinking to speak itself into your heart. The Impostor knows we can only hear from God in the moment. When we are not mind-jammed in all its concerns, we hear with clarity and we are gently guided by grace. This happens naturally, when we know who we are and we walk by faith, letting go into the new moment, to our freedom. The Great I Am is always there. God is in the new moment.

Your Authentic Feelings

Your true feelings are in the moment. They are letting you know what is really going on in the here and now. Once that moment of discernment is missed, you may become oppressed and repressed. Take your moment back and feel your new moment. You can feel through the old feelings into your new moment. Enjoy the ride. Your heart will follow.

Do not be afraid to feel fully and with a depth and a passion. Let the Impostor know you are not afraid to feel, and you refuse to be repressed.

Do not allow the Impostor to persuade you to "not feel" or to be afraid to feel what is going on. If you have the feeling you have received the thoughts, it's a done deal. Now undo the repression, feel with fearlessness and re-think. You will watch your heart open and your consciousness get disentangled. Who you truly are will naturally arise.

The Discerning Heart

Your heart loves to feel. It is a sensitive and a feeling mechanism. The heart's most challenging constriction is that the Impostor always wants to be introspective and wants to bring up thoughts about the past, about the old self. The Impostor wants you to spend your time going within, having you feel, and focus on what it has created with its old baggage. It wants you to focus on the past. Your heart is not interested in this; your heart wants to feel the moment, the environment, music, nature, even the air. Your heart wants to connect with feeling and living outside of your dense generational self.

Your heart wants to share its take on what it knows. It

wants you to hear it. A dog knows by smelling. The heart knows by feeling, by its ability to discern. And it is usually quite accurate.

Denial of feeling is not authority. It is repression and this creates pain and illness in the body. Take your power, mind, and your moment back by undoing the bow with gratefulness, praise, and joy. I like to praise when I am undoing deception while re-thinking and giving thanks. I am grateful I do not have to live in the unconsciousness of the old nature. You will enjoy creating havoc in the mind of the Impostor, and you will be blessed by receiving divine back-up.

Let Go by Faith

In the end, by simply not receiving the mind spin of the Impostor, you will have taken the entire idol down in its entire counterfeit identity. The voice and life of the old nature will have been mortified simply by your walking into the new moment. Let go by faith and a negating of all your thoughts. You do not need to be mindful, but mindless. Do not look back. Surrender deception.

Faith in Integrity

The understanding or resolution of whatever you just walked away from is not as important as the empowering purpose that God has for you, which is to go into the new moment and to have faith in the integrity of the next new moment. When you walk into the new moment by faith, you are laying down the mind control idol and God will reveal to you what you are trying to find out. Let go with all your heart and all your thoughts. It is Holy and magical. Test and see that the Lord is good. Whatever happens in the next new moment, God will deliver you afresh. Expect it and simply walk into the next circumstance by faith and confidence, doubt-free.

Why should you be blamed or concerned? That is exactly what Sin Consciousness is hoping you will acquiesce to, a receptiveness to all its doubt and condemnation. It is in a warfare against you. It is evil. It is a setup to hold you down and push you back. Stay awake in the new moment and God will reveal to you everything you need to know.

Revelation Is on Its Way

Stay open to receiving from circumstances, from friends, from animals. God is using His Universe to speak to you. This is trusting in the Lord with all your heart. This is part of your inherited position in Christ, the grace of the new moment. There are no repercussions in the new moment. There is no oppression for you as you let go of all thought and walk after the spirit, moving on by faith.

Righteousness Consciousness moves in authentic forgiveness and grace. It has nothing to work out. It is already complete in Him. Forgiveness is a quality of the spirit, not a process of the flesh! The Impostor wants to disconnect you from your aliveness, numb you in its agenda of processing its issues. It wants to disconnect you from other people and joy.

> *"I trust in the Lord with all my heart and lean not on my own understanding."*
> —Prov. 3:5

Chapter 19
Righteousness Consciousness and Repressed Love

I have found the best warfare to oppose unconsciousness (fear and doubt) is by going out and connecting from your beautiful heart, choosing to go to your fellow humans with humility, with a consecrated intention of feeling your divine love and seeing God's spirit in all people. Love is a feeling. Often in therapy, people are focused on trying to feel their repressed anger, to release their anger. It can be edifying to do that, as anything is better than being repressed. However, we often forget that there is also repressed love, and a lot of it.

Love is a good feeling, love yourself, your own heart, love God, love your neighbors, feel and share some love. Choose to leave the Impostor behind and go out with the intent to be a blessing.

Your Life Force Is God

The Impostor will bow to your life force. It does not have any life force of its own and it cannot fake it. Death cannot fake life. Your life force has power over all matter. Remove yourself from the Impostor's worried mind. Be a spiritual Zorba the Greek and dance through it. Dancing can be very powerful, more powerful than any spiritual works or study, even better than the works of exercise at the gym. Yes, the unbridled life of dancing has spirit power. I have danced through many body healings. Remember, you have the power of life force and the Impostor has no vibrancy. It is a fake. You do the talking... *"Not now Impostor, I am on to you. No works now."* When you are attacked, go out and live large, dance, hike, sing, love, connect, repeat. Remove yourself from the Impostor's worried mind.

In the bigger spiritual picture, there's only one serious error and that is its "mind spin"—a mind jam. Being seduced into a mind jam is giving the Impostor place, forgetting who you are and allowing it to take your identity, forfeiting your dominion and inheritance, thereby making the power of the Cross and blood of Jesus null and void in your life.

In the new moment, there is only you, free again: The New Creation in Christ, who has always been forgiven, resurrected, redeemed, and reconciled.

The Real Problem Exposed

The problem that you may think you have may not even be the real problem. There is only one problem that could occur. You are not in the new moment in the grace of God. The carnal mind is presenting and representing an alleged problem, an illusion to keep you in its mind jam, hoping that you will "dwell" on it.

The real problem is that you have relinquished your dominion, your separation. You got stuck for a moment in time and you are in a temporary mind jam—no more, no less.

Identify what happened with spiritual insight.

Fighting back and informing the Impostor of your awareness has restoration and elevation power:

> *"I am on to you, Impostor. I have no intention of allowing you to reduce me to a parrot, repeating and going over and over your fears and anxieties."*

> *"I am not trying to figure out what went wrong or how I can fix it. I don't need a fix. I have a separation. I'm fixed."*

> *"I am not bowing to your plan. I refuse to think compulsively and fellowship with your accusations, perceptions, guilt, doubts, or future plans. I have a sound mind…a single mind unto the Lord. This is not my thought."*

> *"So that I come again to my father's house in peace; then shall the LORD be my God"*
> Genesis 28:21

If you find there is still some doubt, if you feel you are not getting the Impostor's thoughts to retreat, there is still a way, even then, to overcome evil.

I Think

Just take over. Take over. Take your mind back. Begin to think consciously. This is more powerful than any meditation. This is simple. Put the Impostor on notice: *"This is my mind, and I am the sole thinker in it. I think. Now shut up."*

Then think. Only one of you can think at a time. Think loud and clear. You may want to begin your "I think" exercise out loud.

Remember that thought creates. Speak your chosen thoughts into your heart. Prophesy and create your heart's desires.

You will experience the power of watching your entire countenance change. You will find what you love, your excitement, your destiny, by "your" thinking.

Watch yourself think and become aware of when your heart is opening, your mood elevating, and your love beginning to naturally exude from your essence.

Think about the territory you are going to take back from the Impostor. Visualize it as it unfolds, piece by piece, break it down from victory to victory.

Think about everybody you know with love. See them as perfect. Think about God's vision for your family, friends, teachers, and coworkers.

> *"Finally, brothers and sisters, whatever is true, whatever is noble, whatever is right, whatever is pure, whatever is lovely, whatever is admirable — if anything is excellent or praiseworthy — think about such things and the God of peace will be with you..."*
> —Philippians 4:8

The Power of Thought

Thinking is the power of the mind. When you think, the God of peace is with you. Often the Impostor is speaking over you, over your heart all day. That is when you feel oppressed and depressed. Beginning today, you are thinking and speaking over it.

Now that you are in your "Holy Identity" you are the chooser and creator of your thoughts, health, and well-being. I like to choose to think first thing in the morning.

The Impostor wants to impart its mental agenda and concerns, the minute your eyes open. It may have been working tenaciously, trying to get the upper hand in your unconscious mind while you slept.

Take control first thing in the morning. Let the Impostor know your purpose, desires, and intents of the day. Express passionately the fruit that you are going to accomplish. Set the creative stage in the mind of the spirit. There is no reason to sit down and watch the Impostor's thoughts. The Impostor must learn to hear and obey your commanding thoughts. Fill your heart with your chosen words and then take the corresponding action by faith. Your heart will rejoice.

Then Now

Even if you were oppressed or misled, even if you were seduced into bowing to the Impostor's plan, after you have taken your mind back, then in the new moment, unencumbered by mental opposition, you will be free to consider what really happened. When you are in Righteousness Consciousness, the truth will naturally unfold. Revelation awaits your return.

The Answer to the Question: What Happened?

The Impostor's favorite diversion is to distract you by continually asking you the question, "What happened?" What happened? What did you do wrong? What went wrong?

This is the opening line to the seduction into the mind jam. It can then add hundreds of scenarios, induce contemplation, and introduce new decisions, things to ponder, consider, and get stuck in. This interrogation is one you want to avoid completely. You could spend hours here, getting blamed, accused, undermined, and disconnected from your life source. Let's face it, God is not in it. Keep your answer to this hook in spiritual fact: You were either misled by the Impostor to a territory, a situation, or a circumstance, for which you were not prepared (not your time or purpose), or you did not guard your heart (take care of yourself), in the new situation that you were led to, or both. Amen.

Your grace is sufficient. Acknowledge your truth and move on. The spirit is naturally correcting, just by your acknowledging the truth. No need to get entangled in self-blame or make promises it will never happen again. All that creates is stress and guilt and it can be more disempowering than fruitful. Do not look back. Grace is always the next new moment of God. It is here now.

The oppression from error does not belong to you. It is a "fear of" making a mistake and then suffering because of it, a fear of punishment. It is an unconscious trigger of fear, remembering your past mistakes, that you have been redeemed from. Do not buy into suffering over an error, a mistake, or being misled. To suffer an error is the Impostor negating the Cross of Calvary and the finished work of Christ in your life. That is a much greater error than any mistake you could possibly accomplish. It is a bow to the idol of mind control.

Redirection

To be led by the spirit is not to be under the law, neither is to be re-led. Re-led is the next new moment of God. Re-direction is better than repentance. It is the obedient and faith-filled action of correcting error. It knows no law, no fear, no past, no Sin Consciousness—it is sacred ground.

Redirect in Jesus' name. There is no old pre-Christ law in heartfelt redirection.

The spirit knows if it can redeem you from your works and your precious lost time, into inspired and creative time. It has the power and authority of choice. Beloved, the spirit in partnership with God will redeem all your wasted time.

The time of the spirit is different. The dispensation of grace has a slower time zone. Love and peace have the power to slow your time down.

> *"A day is a thousand years, unto the Lord,*
> *a thousand years a day."*
> —2 Peter 3:8

You can relax, take a deep breath, smell and see the roses, feel and connect with the cats, pet and receive kisses from the doggies, and enjoy all of God's creations fully. You can dance the dance of your heart and take your sacred moment back. You will also begin to look younger; your spirit is vibrant, youthful, energetic, and radically alive. Your innocence and freedom will return.

This way of being is called "Righteousness Consciousness." I have mentioned this inherited consciousness of Christ many times in this book. Righteousness Consciousness is a radical reliance on spirit, faith, God, and grace.

> "...but the Spirit is life because of righteousness."
> —Rom. 8:10

The spirit person (who you are) knows that a step of faith can elevate it, a step of faith has the power to promote it, resurrect it and empower it. God will work it all out. Do not settle for a morsel, a crumb, from this hateful intellectual idol; do not be defiled from a hand-me-down token of yesterday's manna.

> "For the promise that he would be the heir of the world was not to Abraham or to his seed through the law, but through the righteousness of faith."
> —Rom. 4:13.

Only God Can Raise Your Consciousness

This is the key to all healing. Once you know this, deep down in your heart, you will have power over the Impostor. Its ability to "con"-demn" and deceive you will be limited. Once you truly get this, you are free. You are in the right place at the right time—now, the spirit moment. You will evoke the grace and favor of a very generous God. Your blessings will be lined up waiting for you to receive them. Your cosmic serendipities, connections, and your heart's desires will overwhelm you with joy. You will be appropriating your needs and healings by faith. You have stopped being seduced into adding idols and the works of the Impostor. You will be experiencing all the attributes of your "Holy Identity."

> *"The fruits of the spirit are love, joy, peace, patience, gentleness, goodness, faith."*
> —Gal. 5:22

No Law in Holiness

To be led by the spirit is not to be under the curse of the law, the law of sin and death—it is to be free in "The Perfect Law of Liberty," liberty to partake in all the fruits of the spirit as a beloved child of the Great I Am.

If the law is not present, there are no triggers. There are no triggers in the new creature, as all things have been made new.

Perks of Being You

Being in your "Holy Identity," who you already are, appropriates your divine rights, your spiritual authority on Earth. Your spiritual authority has, within itself, the revelations and the power to solve every problem that you have. Every problem that you have stems from relinquishing your spiritual identity, an unconscious bow to the law in your flesh—no more and no less.

Your God-given spiritual authority has power over the flesh. It has power over the carnal mind, your body, your thoughts, your health, your triggers, and all your past traumas. Without your spiritual authority, you are a lost soul on Earth, a tossed and confused victimized soul reliving the past, powerless over guilt, condemnation, Sin Consciousness, and evil. You could be deceived by the wiles of Sin Consciousness to pay a price that was paid for at the Cross of Calvary, the Impostor's hope fulfilled. You were as prey, were—not anymore.

"That we should no longer be children, tossed to and fro and carried about with every wind of doctrine, by the trickery of men, whereby they lie in wait to deceive."
—Eph. 4:14

Chapter 20

Holy Identity Stand ("HIS")

This is the grace and reality of Jesus Christ. This is authentic Christianity, *sans* dogma, self-righteousness, and mind control. This is your organic Christ within, your Christos in Christos-Sanity. With this new knowledge of your identity and God-given grace to enforce your divine rights, you now have the ability to appropriate your spiritual authority and separate yourself from who you are not. You are ready take a stand! You are who you are, and in your Holy Identity stand, you are "HIS," and all the rest will be added unto you. It already has been, and you will not be denied. You cannot. This is the new law, "The Perfect Law of Liberty." This is the end of doubt, a new fulfilling of who you truly are, the gatekeeper of your mind and the guarder of your heart.

You are now able to take authority over the comments, opinions, beliefs, judgments, and opposing thoughts of the Impostor. This includes the Impostor speaking out of the mouths of those around you: words of friends, TV, Google, etc. Choose what you intend to receive and create.

It is your mind and your life. Choosing that which comes into your heart and soul is throwing the Impostor out. Take back spirit control. Without your spiritual authority, you are not a confident warrior vessel of God. You are, actually, a sitting duck for oppression, a defeated, weak victim of the flesh. You are in the curse of the law: Sin Consciousness, "The Law of Sin and Death." This is the very opposite of your truth, "The Perfect Law of Liberty." The fruit of this deception causes your experience with God to be limited. You will rarely hear, feel, or come into a divine presence. The Law of Sin and Death is perpetually trying to get you involved in another bow, instructing you on how to do something to "improve and heal yourself."

If you are, on occasion, beguiled into giving up your divine rights, as we all are, you can take them back by faith, a demonstration, or a rebuttal. That is the grace of God. This is as good as it can get here on Earth. It is dominion over the old nature. When I declare dominion, I am not just speaking of a "nice" metaphysical moment. I am acknowledging a complete and Radical Redemption, inclusive of a total healing of all your physical diseases and body pains, and a solidification of your mental well-being.

It is your divine right to appropriate your authority for healing, and this is a significant appendage to redemption: a package deal. Sin Consciousness, guilt, victimization, and Condemnation Consciousness will attempt to disempower you in your stand. It will create doubt. It wants to create an idol. It will rise up in Self Exaltation. It wants you to bow to the Impostor. If you do not bow to the Impostor's thoughts within, it will be delighted to have you bow to someone else's Impostor. This is codependency and it is very dangerous to your health.

Permitting this intrusion is simply a lack of understanding of the power of the blood of Christ. The finished work of the Cross is just that "finished." It is done. You are complete in Him. Any undermining of your identity is from "Impostor Consciousness" and its intent to dishonor and negate the redemptive power of Christ and His Cross in your life.

> *"For in Christ all the fullness of the Deity dwells in bodily form. And you have been made complete in Christ, who is the head over every ruler and authority. In Him you were also circumcised in the putting off of your sinful nature, with the circumcision performed by Christ and not by human hands..."*
> —Col. 2:9

If the Impostor is allowed to speak in your mind, it will deny daily the regeneration power of the Holy Ghost. This is the Impostor exalting itself and attempting to make a powerless show of the blood of Jesus. This is the Impostor's self-exaltation and it is utter deception. This is Unholy Ground. You are Holy Ground, the temple of the Most High, not to be contaminated by doubt, but edified by love and faith.

> *"...not by works of righteousness which we have done, but according to His mercy He saved us, through the washing of regeneration and renewing of the Holy Spirit."*
> —Titus 3:5

Assured of Our Identity

Once we come to grips with our true battle, the war between the flesh and the spirit, we understand that Christ has redeemed us from the Law of Sin and Death. We know that Jesus has nothing to do with religion, which is manmade, a fake, created by the Impostor Consciousness itself. When we realize that all agenda, mind control, and condemnation are not the fruits of the spirit, we will switch sides and feel vibrantly alive in Christ. As we begin to perceive the roots and tentacles of "Sin Consciousness" as the very problem that Christ came to conquer, our understanding of our incredible opportunity to transform increases, and we gratefully and humbly chose to stop bowing to deception.

The Grace Bank

You are more than able to do what you are led to do in God's timing. God is preparing you, step by step, to live in the fullness of your purpose in this life, which you are more than able to do, even before you are able to do it. This is borrowing grace from God, the "Grace Bank." A free loan of being the fullness of your "Holy Identity" right now, in this new moment, while you are still attending the School of the Spirit. This very holy process of receiving the "grace loan" from God's Grace Bank, and how you can appropriate it for the healing of your body and mind, will be discussed further in the following chapter on "Divine Retaliation." You will learn how you can cut to the chase of regeneration power and evoke a healing miracle right now.

Once we are assured of our identity and the real war, we begin to gain power over it. Just having the clarity of what is really going on within your mind makes your spiritual resurrection become very tangible, and you will soon be going from a victim mentality to a spiritual reality.

As you begin to express your true self and tell the Impostor who you are, your holy innate spirit power will emerge, set your boundaries on your behalf, and guard your heart. All the feelings, negative thoughts, and fears of the Impostor's manipulations will begin to dissipate right before your eyes.

This is an unforgettable experience and you will never be the same. Your life has just been changed. You have stepped into being you, by your own authority. You will begin to save a lot of money on medications, emergency room visits, doctors, therapy, and self-help. Furthermore, you will be able to arrest a lot of hopelessness and despair that comes from begging for victimizing prayer.

Maintaining Your Holy Identity

To maintain your Holy Identity, you need one simple thing: faith. You can know everything, understand who you are, sing about it, tell others about it, but if you do not walk in it, you will not be able to maintain your truth. This is the part where God will get exactly what He wants. Yes, He is God. You will have to comply with the way that God perceives faith in order to be successful on this journey.

Only God can raise your consciousness; only God can heal you. He does this with faith: your faith.

All of your undesirable situations and circumstances and ailing body parts and illnesses can be eliminated with a step of faith. Faith has the power to open your heart. Faith is larger; it is a spiritual quality and will take a natural dominion over your heart and body. The Impostor will attempt to hold you back from your spiritual authority. It does not want you to appropriate any divine healing of your mind and body, and it desires to block your awareness of the healing power of "Divine Retaliation." The Impostor may have you there right now. Many folks spend half of their life in unnecessary suffering.

The next section of this book will discuss the power of faith in the healing of the body, mind, and soul. You will learn why you may not be appropriating your God-given healing correctly. You will learn how to use the faith of righteousness, violent faith, to get healed, raise your consciousness, transform your mind, and win all your battles, one by one. You will become more of who you truly are, daily, and have your Christos arise. You are about to enter into the supernatural realm of a "Radical Transformational Redemption."

Section III
(Part I)

DIVINE RETALIATION

"The Kingdom of God suffereth violence and the violent shall take it by force."
—Matt. 11:12

Chapter 21
The Healing Power of Divine Retaliation

I cannot write a book about your divine rights and your Holy Identity without introducing the world to the healing power of "Divine Retaliation."

Divine Retaliation Is God's Emergency Room

Spiritual retaliation is the action we take by faith, after we have done all we can do. We choose to embrace our divine authority when we have been ineffective in our attempts to heal on our own, we have added the ways of the world, the doctors, the therapists, the herbalists, perhaps even the prayer warriors, the medications, the meditations, the fasting, the praying, and the studying. I have a list of my own personal efforts and all the things I tried, and it is six pages long. The point is nothing helped me. As a matter of fact, each treatment made me worse. I was not dealing with the real issues, and my denial was further victimizing me. I was moving in a wrong direction, out of purpose and disempowered.

Chapter 22
Violent Faith

Divine Retaliation is a radical reliance on God. It is the process of enforcing your God-given grace. It is the demonstration of knowing who you are in Christ. Divine Retaliation is the human spirit, in obedient action, led by God in its Holy Identity stepping out in violent faith. It is the appropriation of the healing of our bodies, minds, hearts, and spirits with our divine authority in our inherited position of Righteousness Consciousness.

Violent faith is the simultaneous laying down the idols of fear and doubt and dying to the flesh. It is the fullness of the spiritual bulwark, the warrior in Christ. It is how your personal Christos stands firm.

It is a simultaneous surrender and a demonstration of authority; it is an accomplishment that only Jesus can offer. This is where the victory is yours and the battle is the Lord's. Retaliation is voluntarily submitting to the washing and regenerative power of the Holy Ghost. There are no questions or debates in the refining fire of regeneration.

> "Not by the works of righteousness, which we have done, He saved us, but by the washing and regeneration, and renewing of the Holy Ghost."
> —Titus 3:5

Radical Reliance and Regeneration Power

Divine Retaliation is the demonstration of your faith and your willingness to unconditionally agree with God. It is you, as the warrior in Christ, being who you were created to be in the wisdom of God. It is you, the spirit being, knowing that there are battles in this life that only God can win, and that God has won. The sanctified warrior voluntarily goes into the refining fire knowing by faith and revelation that Jesus is always the fourth man in the fire.

> "Without faith it is impossible to please Him; for he that cometh to God must believe that He is, and that He is a rewarder of those who diligently seek Him."
> —Heb. 11:6

The refining fire is where you take your body back from fear and deception; this is the territory where God raises your consciousness to His. It is where you advance in authority and grow in the spirit.

This is where your spiritual power, your anointing for the healing of others, and all your gifts are magnified. This is where your spirit is resurrected. This is the gift of grace that the intellectual mind cannot and will not comprehend. Divine Retaliation will bring the flesh that is opposing you and blocking you from moving ahead under subjection. It is stand healing. It is using your divine rights in The Perfect Law of Liberty and your identity in Righteousness Consciousness to appropriate the healing that was given to you at the Cross.

This is where the Holy Spirit moves on your behalf as a child of God; this is where your Christos rises up by doing what it came to do.

> *"Wherefore take unto you the whole armor of God, that ye may be able to withstand in the evil day, and having done all, to stand."*
> —Eph. 6:13

This is where you receive revelation, where you have an encounter with Christ, and where you have the actual experience of being who you truly are. Your anointing and gifts are not evoked or empowered from teachings or seminars. They can only come from *your personal step of faith*. This is the one, my brothers and sisters, that the church does not have a seminar for.

> *"Be not deceived; God is not mocked: for whatsoever a man soweth, that shall he also reap."*
> —Gal. 6:7

Chapter 23
The Cross of Love

I am not talking about self-will. I am not talking about trying to make something happen. I am talking about literally falling on the grace of God. Being who we truly are is our greatest worship unto the Lord. It is appreciating what He has accomplished at the Cross of Calvary and acknowledging it in a very mature way. This is the definition of spiritual humility: laying down who we are not and accepting our authority and our spiritual inheritance of dominion on Earth.

This is the sanctifying and refining process of dying to the generational self. As you are separating yourself from the beliefs of the Impostor's Counterfeit Consciousness, you are simultaneously overcoming the old nature's innate victimizations.

You are enforcing your Holy Identity by overcoming the Sin Consciousness identity of the old nature. Christ overcame it for you at the Cross and you are in agreement by your demonstration of violent faith.

This is how we win. This is believing the Word of God, the promises of God, and accepting the Cross of Christ as a completed work and an overcoming weapon for you to stand on. It is making the Word of God a reality in your life. This is not the

Cross of religion or Sin Consciousness that dictates judgment, fear, guilt, or punishment. This is the Cross of personal empowerment, available and willing to embrace, include, and protect every person on Earth—the Cross of love.

> *"In Him we have redemption through*
> *His blood, the forgiveness of our sins,*
> *according to the riches of his grace."*
> —Eph. 1:7

Chapter 24
Conquering Doubt

A spiritual retaliation has within itself the inherent resurrection power to change your thoughts, consciousness, and all your perceptions. We are far too often shut down by doubt. Doubt may be calling your bluff, arresting your ability to move ahead with the Impostor's generational consciousness, and using fear triggers that no longer belong to you.

> *"Therefore if any man be in Christ, he is a new creature: old things are passed away; behold, all things are become new."*
> —2 Cor. 5:17

These triggers no longer belong to you because they are part of the old creature's past from which you were redeemed. Have you ever been in a battle you cannot win? You try and try, but you always seem to end up in the same place, sick, disgusted, and hopeless. Have you been in a battle that overwhelms you? I have. I have been in battles so over my head that even stepping in closer with fasting and prayer became a setback. Prayer is not moving ahead! After you pray, you stand against deception! After you have done all you can do, stand!

> *"Therefore take up the whole armor of God, that you may be able to withstand in the evil day, and having done all, to stand!"*
> —Eph. 6:13

Lying Symptoms

Doubt can create lying symptoms and aggressive, intimidating and fearful thoughts, and create a trigger-oriented hyper-defensive self-protecting, and reactive consciousness, one that proliferates body pain and tension. Many have lost battles by not understanding that the process of retaliation is not through religious faith, but violent faith. Sometimes, the unconscious mind is not yet sufficiently sanctified and can create a great resistance to your overcoming the symptoms and weaknesses of the flesh.

The "Doing What You Cannot Do" Belief

The Impostor will trick you into believing that faith is doing something that you cannot do. The Impostor wants to make your "stand" a passive stance. It is not. It is the stand of the spirit; it is the action of violent faith! For example, if you are allergic to milk and you drink a glass of milk, according to the Impostor, you are a great faith walker. You are rocking your faith. This is "Impostor Consciousness." The truth is, the Impostor has set you up for defeat. You are a sitting duck for a huge reaction. The Impostor is about to take more from you. This evil enemy is about to kick you when you are down, when you are sick. The Impostor wants your territory, your hope, and, most importantly, your faith. You cannot fight the impostor on its territory. You cannot do a little of what you are unable to do and get a healing. You are not making your point.

Fake Faith

For instance, let's say you are allergic to carrots and you decide to take them back by faith. You have decided to do what you cannot do: eat a carrot by faith and take back the carrot. This appears to be faith, as you are doing what you are unable to do. But it is not faith. You will not be met there. This is not how God sees faith. This is not the faith of a hip spiritual warrior in Righteousness Consciousness. This is the faith of religion trying to make a show of itself with one carrot, looking good to the religious believer, but it is the Impostor setting you up for a fall and faking faith.

The Impostor has used and created this system of religious faith to toss you into doubt and defeat. The Impostor will attack your foods and have you react to the one carrot you are trying to reinstate into your diet. It may attack other parts of your body, creating back pain, nausea, and other lying symptoms to attack your faith. It will use "fear of" getting worse, it will threaten you that you are creating physical damage to your body. It will use doubt to push you back even further than where you were to begin with. Instead of gaining faith and having a victory, you will have faith taken from you. The Impostor has its evil and primitive eyes on your territory. To the Impostor your move ahead is its disempowerment.

Then, the Impostor will follow up with a second punch

and create an opportunity to add some condemnation by using an always available religious interpretation: "You cannot tempt God, God doesn't heal everyone... God heals who He wants to heal." I have often heard that God just does not heal anymore. These are the perceptions of doubt, self-exaltation, religion, mind control, error, and more doubt. There are many available prophets of doubt for the Impostor to employ, but this is not the edifying voice of the spirit. The spirit speaks in the language of faith.

The Impostor's counterfeit mentality is in direct opposition to your redemption. It desires to make the Cross of Christ without healing power in your life. The truth is, you are healed. God has healed you. It is an already done deal. Now it is your turn, your job, to bring the flesh under subjection. To do this, you have to know who you are.

> *"The spirit is willing, but the flesh is weak"*
> —Matt. 26:41

Grace Bank Loan

This is when you apply by faith for the loan from the Bank of Grace. This is when you cannot, on your own, achieve your desired healing, even when you know and believe that you are truly healed. However, when you are still feeling overwhelmed by the deceptions of Counterfeit Consciousness, you need more Christos, more spirit power.

Divine Retaliation evokes the grace that is by faith, now,

when you need it. We activate the grace of God by our spiritual faith and knowledge. Righteousness is an action of the Spirit. Righteous action is stepping out, taking the action of faith against the belief, and immobilizing "fear" in the old nature.

You will begin to notice that much of what you have been taught to believe and to accept as your reality is not true and much of what you may have considered to be a physical problem, or an illness, has absolutely nothing to do with your body. This will be a life-changing and empowering connection to make.

Sometimes, this revelation requires hitting your personal rock bottom and then subsequently making a decision to give it all to God. As a matter of fact, the more impossible the situation is, the more grace power you will get when you step out and confront your circumstance. That is the irony of spiritual healing.

> *"Where therefore I take pleasure in infirmities, in reproaches, in necessities, in persecutions, in distresses for Christ's sake: for when I am weak, then am I strong."*
> —2 Cor. 12:10

If you can do it yourself, you do not need the grace of God!

Chapter 25
Decomposing Trauma

Divine Retaliation in the spirit can be described as an upping of the ante and a pushing of deception back by "violent faith." You do this by showing and knowing who you are, by confronting fears—beliefs that are held deep in the unconscious carnal mind, fears that do not belong to your true nature, fear triggers from your past, and generationally inherited fears.

These fears are locked into our bodies, creating lying symptoms, chronic pain, chronic illnesses, false beliefs, anxieties, the restimulation of trauma, and repressed emotions. They will reveal their dark and ugly heads as we oppose and provoke them. They are just bullying deceptions and will come under your subjugation as you demonstrate your faith and knowledge. These fear beliefs are being used to pull you out of the spirit. You are the one that must bring these unconscious fears to naught and make them bow to your God-given authority.

You are a divine warrior here on Earth. As you walk toward these battles and confront these fleshly manifestations by faith, you will gain resurrection spirit power.

The truth is you already have power over them. However, you will have to rise up in the spirit and confront them to truly know that and to establish your position of dominion over them.

The Short Cut to Transformation

Divine Retaliation is inner healing. It is getting at the root of the trigger or trauma in one fell swoop. It is evoking the revelation that will come later, after the physical healing, when you have the luxury of spiritual growth.

As you consecrate to solving your dilemmas in God's plan, by authentic faith, the faith of the spirit, you are dying to the old self, the old self that has the issue from which you have been redeemed. The problem no longer belongs to you in your Holy Identity. As you stand firm and are no longer tossed from your "incorruptible seed," you are becoming more of your true identity, less of the old nature, and more of your Christos, who is already healed.

A Bluff Call

You have already won. The Lord has empowered you and now the triggers, trauma, and fears of the old nature will all bow as long as you do not bow. It is a bluff call. As in any good card game, when we call the bluff of our opponent, we raise the stakes and we up the ante.

Without raising the stakes, it is difficult to convince your opponent that you know you have a winning hand. Your trump card is the blood of Jesus and you can call upon it at any time in the battle. Calling upon it and not being in the actual battle is often the old creature, and you may not get the response you are seeking.

Talking and not walking can be fear and doubt holding you back with an erroneous belief that confessing without action is sufficient. When you see yourself being pushed back, stressed out, or immobilized by fear, know this is not you—this is a trigger of the flesh. It is just fear coming from the old nature. Do not relinquish your territory.

If you cannot clearly see where your retaliation move is, move in closer to it, and God will release the revelation. You can see more by faith than the wisest person in the world.

> *"He will use the foolish things of this world to confound the wise."*
> —1 Cor. 1:27

Stepping Out in Divine Retaliation

As you step out in your Divine Retaliation, your situation may appear to be the same, but your power changes. You change. When you are stepping out in your Holy Identity, you are doing what the mind of fear and doubt does not want you to do, exactly what doubt is afraid to do, and precisely what it is telling you that you can't do. In the realm of matter, in the laws of mortal man, without the awareness of your spiritual authority, you cannot do it. Fear is relying on your ignorance.

Just when fear thinks it has you bowing to it, just as fear creates a lying symptom (a symptom that you may have allowed yourself to be pushed back from and overcome by in the past) in that very moment, you will add more of exactly what doubt and fear are telling you will cause you harm. In that very moment, as you are being threatened and intimidated into relinquishing your divine rights, you will be led by God to bring the flesh that is opposing you under subjection. Violent faith is using your divine rights in The Perfect Law of Liberty and your identity in Righteousness Consciousness to enforce the healing that was given to you at the Cross.

Blowing the Mind of Doubt

As you oppose fear by upping the ante and adding more of exactly what you are being threatened to not do, you will blow doubt's mind! A warrior knows you cannot conquer fear in the mind, which is its exalted territory; you must up the ante on fear, until it bows to you. Notice, I did not suggest you step out do what you cannot do. This is the trap. Using the seductive belief that doing what you can't do is faith. I suggested to you to do what doubt, fear, and all its intimidating and aggressive thoughts are telling you that you cannot do. Oppose these hostile suggestions and then add a little more opposing action, often a lot more, and keep adding territory until doubt and self-exaltation bow to you. That is the difference between religious faith and violent faith. Violent faith holds nothing back! The redeemed spirit opposes the Holding-Back-Syndrome of doubt and condemnation with its Holy Identity.

Changing Your Reality

As you retaliate the Impostor's attacks on your body, mind, and soul, and move ahead of its threats, you will gain spirit power. Doubt and self-exaltation are always attempting to push you back, making you smaller than who you are called to be by taking your territory. You have a divine right and a supreme ordinance to take your territory back. Once you make your faith decision to move in your right direction, everything will begin to change. Actually, everything will change immediately. You are now in the real battle: the war between the flesh and the spirit. You are in the war that you are predestined to win.

You are not in denial of your identity. You are not chasing devils that were overcome at the Cross. You are not in therapy discussing the old creature's problems, you are not home studying, you are on the front line in the fire with Jesus. You will get what you came to get and so much more in sanctification, enlightenment, revelation, and a vibrant intimacy with Christ. You are in the resurrection power of the Holy Ghost! You are in a "Radical Transformational Redemption." You are pleasing unto the Lord. You will be the recipient of divine favor!

Chapter 26
Restoration via Retaliation

Whatever you may have relinquished in your life, wherever you may have previously given your power away due to the seductive influence of the enemy of your spirit, all can be rapidly restored by a righteous spiritual battle and confrontation. This is inclusive of all your spiritual fruits: peace, joy, love, authority over body pain, and divine health. If oppression has reigned in your life for a season, you may have to begin by beating it back with a "Divine Retaliation." A notice, a watch, a rebuke, or a conversation may not be sufficient. Truly, it is all territorial in the spiritual realm. It is a primal battle. We have often become too complex and sophisticated to perceive it.

Dying to the Old Self

This is the process of dying in Christ. It is not a silent meditation, but rather a front-line confrontation of our flesh and the opposition that it creates to our surrender and authority in Christ.

Do not blame yourself—you are exactly where you are supposed to be.

> *"But I see another law in my members, warring against the law of my mind, and bringing me into captivity to the law of sin which is in my members."*
> —Romans 7:23

Making Fear Bow to You

The power of faith healing is to vehemently confront the opposition—to make fear bow to you. The truth of faith healing is that you, as the spirit person, by your position as the Righteousness of God in Christ, are already healed. You have two choices: you can be tempted and then bow to the fear and doubt perceptions of the Impostor or you can confront them. Once you know who you are, you will joyfully confront these intimidating perceptions.

Reversing Fear Triggers

The spirit's way to arrest the triggers, which are creating the lying symptoms in your body and mind, is to *stop bowing to them*. You cannot redo your childhood; you cannot cut fear triggers and their memory out of your brain. However, as you stop allowing them to victimize you, as you increase in the spirit, you will become detached from them. You will be larger in your Christos than the triggers are in your fear mind. Your heart will not shut down ("be triggered" by fear) when you are not intimated or limited by it, when you not only don't buy the lie, but you reverse the game, and step out with violent faith and take your power back from these hostile and erroneous intimidations.

When you understand this, it becomes your opportunity for a radical promotion in the spirit. You will begin to volunteer to take more of your territory back. You will take back what fear is trying to take from you, and soon you will be excited and inspired to take more. You will show fear who you truly are, not by words, but by your actions and by your demonstration of violent faith.

You are literally speaking to fear by your demonstration. You are saying loud and clear: *"I have had all I am going to tolerate. This time, Impostor, you will bow. This time, you will pay—my healing is paid for. As a matter of fact, fear, every time that you dare to oppose me, from this day forth, I will be inspired to the next reclamation of my power. You will lose more territory than you gain. I have God-given authority over you. You will decrease, and I will increase, and my mind will be exorcized of fear and doubt, by my violent faith."*

> *"And He cast out spirits with His Word..."*
> —Matt. 8:16

Healing of the Heart

One of the many perks of your physical healing is the healing of your heart. You, the warrior spirit, are actually guarding your heart and taking care of yourself as you confront fear. Your heart is no longer abandoned and available for downloads of terror. It is sheltered in your protection and no longer subject to the rubbish of doubt and condemnation. It is secure and guarded. Trust has been resorted. You have been naturally elevated by faith to sit above the carnal mind in Righteousness Consciousness, as an awakened chooser of what you will receive. Divine Retaliation connects you to your pure Christos power and then takes you directly to the root of the issue it is correcting. Jesus is an incredible psychiatrist, healer, deliverer and sanctifier, all in one…

Chapter 27

Confronting with Your Christos

There is a reason why only violent faith has power in the battle. Let's go back to our one carrot example. The Impostor knows you might get sick eating one carrot, but you will not die. You are not really confronting fear. You are tapping it on the shoulder, saying, *"Hello, I am here, attempting to take your Kingdom down, but I'm really uncertain if you are the real problem, a part of me still believes I have food allergies, that I have my illness, that I am my body, and that this is a physical issue...I am not totally convinced that I am immortal spirit, and holy. I'm not certain God will meet me."*

If any of these ideas are similar to your perceptions, you are negotiating, not demanding. You are not a threat. The Impostor quickly assesses your position and knows that you do not know who you are. The Impostor concludes that you have been misinformed and it plots against you to gain more territory.

You must be willing to die here, to die to the beliefs of the flesh. At the same time, know that your spirit will arise. Violent faith is faith in the blood of Christ, rescuing you from the fire, being the fourth man in your situation.

> *"He answered and said, Lo, I see four men loose,
> walking in the midst on the fire, and they have no hurt,
> and the form of the fourth is like the Son of God."*
> —Daniel 3:25

> *"For to me to live is Christ, and to die is gain."*
> —Philippians 1:21

Fear: What Do You Have?

One carrot is not the refining fire. One carrot is a candle burning in the wind of doubt. Imagine a card game. You are about to call the bluff of evil by upping the ante on your opponent. Let fear know you are not buying its hand!

> *"Fear, what do you have? You have a belief in food allergies; you believe that I agree with you, that I have an allergy to carrots."*

> *"Impostor, you have carrots. You have a threat that I will react to carrots and get sick. You have a one carrot card, a one carrot bet; I have reacted to one carrot in the past; I have bowed to carrots."*

> *"My position has changed. I no longer bow to carrots or anything else. I have faith that I am a healed woman, that I was healed at the Cross of Calvary, and this is all a lie, an attack on my identity. It is a*

Section III: (Part I) Divine Retaliation

deception, a con job. I know that it is you creating lying symptoms in my body—you the flesh, you Impostor, will come under the subjection to the Lordship of Jesus Christ. You will bow to my authority. I will eat what I want to eat. I will go where I want to go. I will do what I want to do. I am the Righteousness of God in Christ, in The Perfect Law of Liberty."

"I will eat ten carrots. I am not afraid of carrots. I am not afraid of you or your alleged power. I know there is no power but the power of God. If you create a lying symptom when I eat ten carrots, I will add milk; I will drink two bottles of milk. You are convinced I am more allergic to milk than carrots. That is your belief, it does not belong to me!

If you create a lying symptom to the milk I drink, I will then eat every food I have ever reacted to, all of it. I am done with this bluff. I will go as far as I must to push you back. You will die, flesh. Fear, you will die. And doubt, you will bow, and I will live! Kill me if you can, Impostor. I don't think you can; you have food, but I have the blood of Jesus. I know I have the trump card!"

Come On, Christos

"Let's go. I'll back you up so far, that you will never oppose me again. This time, you will bow. I am done. I'll continue to take more territory. I'll push you so far

back you will lose all your territory today, as I up the ante on your illusions. You will encounter Jesus today Imposter, He will be the fourth man in the fire."

Going on Up

This is where you will go, up—this is how God perceives faith. The Lord knows He is always the fourth man in the fire. He wonders what we are waiting for, why we are sitting around fasting, praying, crying out, begging, worshipping...for what the Great I Am, has already given us.

Real worship takes the territory and mortifies the deeds of the flesh.

"For if ye live after the flesh, ye shall die: but if ye through the Spirit do mortify the deeds of the body, ye shall live."
—Rom. 8:13

Faith Is Not Just One Carrot

Faith is not just one carrot or doing what you cannot do. It is bringing the opposition to your freedom under subjection. It is violent faith, the faith of the Righteousness of God—Holy Faith. You will feel the presence of God after you have taken fear down and made a show of it. Faith is conquering fear, at the root of the lie, by being who you already are. Faith takes the fear bully down, calling it out. Faith declares, *"Then kill me if you can; you don't back me up."* If you cannot say that and mean it, fear will not bow.

I have tested the system. I have personally done this process with every food group, mold spore, and toxic chemical on the planet. I have done it with torn ligaments and disabled body parts. I have done it with life threatening illnesses and circumstances. It is all the same!

I have stood with hundreds of clients to take their territory back in this very battle, the battle of the war between the flesh and the spirit. The only way you can be defeated in this battle is to not up the ante on deception, to allow yourself to be pushed back to victimization and doubt, thereby relinquishing your identity. Doing so is a tremendous defeat for the spirit. It is despair. It is the flesh exalting itself above the power of God.

Chapter 28

Laying the Idols Down

Remember, it is the bow that created the problem in the first place, no more and no less. It is undoing the bow that will correct the error. Undoing the bow is the healing of your situation, laying the idols down. If you do not allow fear and doubt to control your mind and hold you back, you will win. Faith healing, my brothers and sisters, is upping the ante on deception and then taking your spirit power back from the flesh and laying the idols down. I will say it again. Faith healing is simply laying the idols down. It is the very opposite of adding the idols of works, teachings, ritualistic prayers, or procrastinating with mind spins—it is laying the idols down. There is nothing new here. Are you getting this? If you are getting this, you are gaining a new respect and reverence for your Creator. You are about to bow in the right direction. Your spiritual consciousness and your power are about to be raised, not by a seminar, but by the Lord Himself, by the one who is able.

Remember the Card Game

"What do you have, Impostor? You have one carrot and a glass of milk... I raise you, by ten carrots... You have a lying symptom of stomach pain. I add two bottles of milk. I raise you. I take more. I will drink two bottles of milk and add a Coca Cola—what do you have now? A headache to throw in the pot—I raise you: beef jerky, French fries, wheat bread, and a steak. As a matter of fact, Impostor, I am adding everything I am allergic to, everything you are telling me I am allergic to, everything you want me to believe I have been allergic to, everything you are telling me will kill me or cause me terrible irreversible damage. You have a death threat; I have the blood of Jesus. You will die, but I will live and be radically alive. I am a healed spirit woman. You are a deception, a bully. There is no way I will bow to you. You will bow to me, now, today."

I am sharing a simple version of a primal spiritual battle, a violent faith battle that can give you the victory over any illness, body pain, or disease. He uses the foolish things of this world to confound the wise. I was healed of lupus by laying the idols down and standing against deception with violent faith! Lupus is an allegedly incurable disease...

> *"But God hath chosen the foolish things of the world to confound the wise; and God hath chosen the weak things of the world to confound the things which are mighty."*
> —1 Corinthians 1:27

How to Be Met by God

This is the answer to the "where is God?" doubt cry of the flesh. When we retaliate, we will be met and elevated by God. We will know where God is. He is with you waiting for you to walk toward your territory. You will have an adventure with Christ, a personal encounter with God, by faith. It is the law of faith.

You will not be met because you are "saved" or tithe or pray every day. You will not be met because you are a nice person. You will be met when you step out and are willing to lay down the belief, the deception, the apprehension, the anger, the diagnosis, the medications, the pain, and the lying symptoms of the old nature. You will be met when you choose to step out by faith *anyhow* and activate your dominion and grace by the demonstration of your spiritual authority. This is true even if you do not have any spiritual authority yet. This is how you get it. It is the spirit's on-the-job training experience.

Chapter 29
A Powerful Weapon

There is nothing in the warrior's arsenal as powerful as Divine Retaliation. As a matter of fact, I was healed of Lupus and Environmental Illness by the grace and power of God while stepping out in the aggressive faith of Divine Retaliation. I was led to violently retrieve my health through the understanding and knowledge of my spiritual identity.

I had to confront fear through Divine Retaliation, with a demonstration of my spiritual authority, and take my Kingdom back. It makes both perfect logical and primal sense once you are able to perceive it with the insight of the spirit. Doubt and fear create a bow, a giving up of our power. If you give up your nutrition, as I did (with a fear-based belief in allergies), the very substance that keeps your body alive, you have bowed your essence to fear, and your spirit will become oppressed.

This is easy to comprehend. The reversal of that subjugation is the restoration and resurrection of the real you, your spirit, by undoing the bow. This will evoke the regeneration and resurrection power of God to meet you in a stand. It is a spiritual law: You will be met. The Holy Spirit, the anointing of God, will break the power of the yoke of bondage.

Often God will allow prayer to heal us for a season; prayer and deliverance ministry can be the carrot of God. Ultimately, God wants you to grow up and overcome the old nature and stop the bow. It is inevitable. Why go through life moving from one type of victimization to another?

> *"Stand fast therefore in the liberty wherewith*
> *Christ hath made us free and be not entangled*
> *again with the yoke of bondage."*
> —Galatians 5:1

Chapter 30
The Holding-Back Syndrome

You will be met as you walk by faith, and faith, of course, requires action. You will not be healed waiting on the Lord for the perfect time; you will not and have not been healed, relaxing in the peace of God, or by spending all your time praying, fasting, and studying more. If that were true, you would be healed by now. That is doubt holding you back with a spirit of procrastination.

This is called the "The Holding-Back Syndrome." It is a manipulation of fear and doubt to keep you out of the healing action of your faith, to keep you out of your spiritual aliveness, your purpose and your life. The Impostor knows only violent faith can conquer it. You cannot overcome the Impostor on the territory of the carnal mind. It is simply more mind; you have been deceived to relinquish your divine power. It is like going to a nuclear war with a pistol. You are not equipped to handle your generational triggers while you are still attached to them.

A Faith Decision

Once I made my decision to take my initial stand, I had an immediate victory, one that I desperately needed. God's comment was, "What took you so long?" I had waited until I was sixty pounds, dying, and tormented. For what? For fear and doubt to oppress and intimidate me further! I did not have the knowledge I needed. I simply did not know my rights. Although I must confess, I had urges. I often thought I should just fill my refrigerator up with food and eat.

The Spirit Knoweth All Things

In the depth of your being, you know exactly what you want to do, what you need to do, and what God has called you to do. The more that you eliminate fear, the more your innate knowing is unblocked. This is how we hear from our Creator. This is how He expects us to be in an intimate relationship with Him and be led by Him and by faith. He is, after all, the God of Faith.

Chapter 31
High in the Christos

As you demonstrate your true identity by spiritually confronting whatever is holding you back, the revelation you have been seeking is unblocked. It was always available to you, and now you can receive it. You are sitting in Christ, high in the Christos, where your spirit always was. You have literally pushed the force that was blocking it out of your way.

The Impostor might be thinking in your mind, right now, *"She's crazy, you cannot be certain when God will meet you... Who does she think she is?"*

The Law of Faith
However, this is a law: The Law of Faith.

> *"Where is boasting then? It is excluded. By what law? Of works? Nay: but, by the law of faith. Therefore, we conclude that a man is justified by faith and without the deeds of the law."*
> —Rom. 3:26

Justified by Faith, Not Fake

When I was allergic to foods, there was not one food that I was not reactive to. A drink of purified water would create blisters in my mouth and rashes all over my body. This was diagnosed as a "Universal Reactor," someone who cannot eat or drink anything without severe allergic reactions. I could no longer survive in the world when I had my initial encounter with Christ. I had not eaten a morsel of food in days. I was living in the mountains of Santa Barbara in isolation, with windows foiled and tightly shut. No light, no air, and no furniture. No one could enter my non-toxic wood shack, and I was not able to leave. I had become the "bubble girl."

I knew very little about spiritual healing. I was a beginner in spiritual knowledge and treated as such. At first, when I had my initial encounter with Jesus, I was healed by grace. I was raised from the near dead, and I experienced an NDE and a miracle healing simultaneously.

After my first life-sparing God encounter, my healing occurred in increments. I would learn more, receive a new revelation, go up a notch, and gain a deeper understanding of the real battle I was facing, and receive more grace. This would bring more ability to eat, more power to digest more food, and more health. Then I would be able to tolerate more foods and be around more chemicals, ones that were, in the past, toxic to me. Soon I was able to come out of my isolation and leave my house.

Piece by Piece

Piece by piece, I was being restored. I was certain I would go all the way, a little here, a little there, more and more grace. I was surrendering my beliefs, my thoughts, my ways, all that I used to be, and with each surrender, I would get a little closer to God and receive more healing, more Jesus. It was a beautiful, sacred, and loving walk with God.

Why Was I Sick?

However, there were reasons why I was ill. They were reasons that had absolutely nothing to do with food, chemicals, allergens, my immune system, or my body parts. My physical reactions were not the root of my dysfunction. My real issues were not food, and neither were they environmentally nor physically derived.

The Real Issues

I soon discovered there were "triggers" that would emerge as I was walking out my healing. There were idols, the old nature's baggage and ways of the generational past. I was learning to surrender to my position of being a healed woman in the spirit. It was a complete and total surrender. It was not an overnight healing—it was a process of a radical transformation, by the grace of God.

Chapter 32
The Redirection

After my initial encounter with a loving Christ, I was certain I would go all the way. I was happy for the first time in my life; I had true joy. I had no reason to believe anything else. I was alive, raised from the dead. Who was I to doubt? However, something else was going on, something I did not understand at all, something I did not know existed.

I was in the war between the flesh and the spirit. I would lose my healing and then God would heal me again, countless times, over and over. I would gain power, lose power, gain three foods just to lose two until finally the Lord spoke to me and changed the direction in which my healing was going to proceed.

These were His exact words: *"My daughter, I am not healing you or delivering you anymore. You will take it by faith with your authority in Christ. If you do not take it by faith, you will never have anything. Every gain you make will be taken away from you; you will always be in a battle for your health and peace. Your problem is not allergies to foods, it is not your reactions to chemicals, it is not immune dysfunction or lupus—your problem is 'powerlessness,' and if you do not retrieve your power, you will never hold on to your healing."*

Addicted to Victimization

I had two kinds of power to take back. I had no strength at that time to reconcile my emotional integrity. That would come later. I first needed a body. I would first have to mature in my spiritual integrity. I had entered into God's emergency room of grace. I was very excited and grateful to hear the words of a new plan, a redirection to empower me. I had just lost another battle, and I was experiencing one of many of my ups and downs. I was scared and utterly alone, and I was becoming discouraged and tired of "trying" to hold on to my healing.

The Impostor's hold on me was very strong. I had given up a lot of territory. I had been backed up and reduced to sixty pounds. The spirit of victimization had fully immobilized me.

I was learning more truth daily, but I had gone so far down, a lifetime of repeating generational compromises. I simply did not have the power to stop it. I had an addiction to victimization and powerlessness. The Impostor could take me down and oppress me like an undertow at sea. I could watch it, feel it, know what it was doing, and yet still be overwhelmed. It was so attached to me that I did not have the strength to arrest its hold.

At first, I was delighted when God spoke. I was encouraged to have a new plan. I went to bed joyful and inspired. But in the light of day, in the morning, I got up thinking, "Hey, wait a minute. Just what authority are we talking about? I am losing more foods, I can hardly eat, I am still allergic to all chemicals, I am stuck, I am sick. Hey, hello, I need a healing." Sound familiar? God had a plan.

Victim Mentality to Spiritual Reality

Jesus was about to show me who I truly was and how to demonstrate to my opposition (fear) that I was my Holy Identity and I was not available for any past fears, doubts, or victimizations. I had divine authority, power that needed to be ignited by faith and by faith alone. I would have to learn how to appropriate all the healings that I had been trying to hold on to by utilizing my violent faith. I was about to be taken out of a state of mortal powerlessness, out of being beaten down, out of a lifetime of generational victimization, to my own personal spiritual reality and power.

Chapter 33
Dominion on Earth

God was about to teach me how to win and how to uphold "Righteousness Consciousness," dominion on Earth. Dominion on Earth, my friends...I am not talking about a meditation, a teaching, a Bible study, or the afterlife. I am not speaking hypothetically or metaphysically. Yes, dominion on Earth—no hype, no pie in the sky or false promises. Actual dominion on Earth is yours to apprehend by faith, today!

The Favor of God

This fact will shake up some hidden religious beliefs. This could be a good time to tune in and separate yourself from the "thoughts" of a faithless Impostor, the doubt-and fear-ridden Impostor that is opposing your grand spirit. Watch it go crazy and then tell it who you are. There are many people who enjoy pontificating about their spiritual achievements, "Oh yes, we have dominion on Earth." However, it is walking and demonstrating, rather than pontificating, that evokes the favor of God.

I am talking about not needing hospitals, not having illness nor depression, nor addictions. I am talking about having your own authority over your mind, heart, and health. I am speaking of your being free to achieve the purpose you came here to accomplish. What is the Impostor thinking now? Are you ready to mortify the deeds of the flesh?

> *"For if ye live after the flesh, ye shall die:*
> *but if ye through the Spirit do mortify the deeds*
> *of the body, ye shall live."*
> —Rom. 8:13

In the next section, I will share a variety of testimonies of Divine Retaliation, so that you may gain a better understanding of this healing process. I believe it is much easier to get the revelation by reading the testimonies than by my trying to impart the "how to." These will be simple and brief Divine Retaliations. There have been many more lengthy and significant retaliations. There have been many Divine Retaliations that have conquered long-standing and terminal illnesses, such as my own. However, they are more complicated with diverse and lengthy tales. These will be the essence of my next book — let's add your story! Let God know you are available, "You provide the fire Lord, I will bring the sacrifice."

My personal retaliations about my healing from lupus, environmental illness, chronic fatigue syndrome, and Epstein Barr virus are in my testimony book, *"Enforcing Grace."* The stories I am about to share are compiled of simple ways and situations that will help make the violent faith process of upping the ante on deception easy to comprehend and utilize for your own personal healing demonstrations.

Section III
(Part II)

VICTORIOUS TALES OF DIVINE RETALIATION

Chapter 34
Jane's Story of Conquering Food Allergies

For my first story of a testimony of Divine Retaliation, I will share Jane's account of how she retrieved her foods with violent faith and an understanding of the divine healing power of an authentic spiritual battle.

You will see the simplicity of how Jane conquered her illness by faith and how she was able to overcome fifteen years of suffering and disability in twenty-four hours. Really in one hour, Jane was healed.

Jane was a hairdresser in Los Angeles and had worked with toxic chemicals all her life. The Impostor's claim was, that because Jane had been exposed to a daily dose of toxicity for years, that she was now suffering from an immune system suppression and was allergic to all foods and many chemicals. This was the Impostor's unwavering story.

Jane had been attending my healing services in Los Angeles for about a year, and her faith was increasing from hearing the truth of her identity and the witnessing and partaking in the healing of others at the meetings.

One morning, she approached me after the service and shared that her allergies had become so intensified, she had to quit her job. She was desperate and very willing to take her stand. She had reached the point of disgust. She was done.

She was being pushed back from her work, and her life was becoming very limited. All she could digest at this point was tuna fish. She was down to being able to eat only one food without severe reactions.

Relinquishing Territory

This is always what the Impostor does: gives you a story, a rationale of why you are disabled, in pain and de-energized. Then, if you are receptive to its deceptive tale, it proceeds to take more territory. The Impostor will take everything you are willing to give up away from you. It does this by threatening you. The Impostor had been threatening Jane with each food that she would attempt to eat, until she was intimidated into giving it up. The Impostor had begun its dietary restrictions with a warning to Jane to not eat bread. "A piece of bread has mold in it, which would worsen her Candidiasis. A piece of bread has wheat, so it would increase her gluten sensitivities." The Impostor then attacked a glass of milk, *"Don't drink milk, as milk has lactose, and it will give you a headache, etc."*

The Impostor would systematically do this with every food Jane ate. It added the latest medical fear, the disease of the hour, the illness *du jour*, the trendy medical tale, to magnify her unconscious hidden fear beliefs. The Impostor systematically eliminated every food group until she was down to one food: tuna fish. It is always the same technique the Impostor uses with every inflicted person. The warfare tactics are always very similar. The Impostor sows fear and doubt; torment is received, and corresponding painful physical symptoms are created, and territory is thereby relinquished. If I say territory relinquished or creating an idol, in the spiritual realm, it is one and the same! Codependency and idolatry are the same thing. A bow by any other name is still a bow! Once you stop thinking as a victim, as an alleged sinner, you can begin to perceive the bigger picture and discern what is really happening. You are bowing to whom you are not.

Jane Decides to Stand

At this point of desperation, at her personal rock bottom, and having heard a lot of truth, Jane was fully convinced that this was her time to take a stand. She asked me to be her guide, to facilitate her stand. Standing with a brother or sister is my favorite thing to do in this world. I know I am about to see a move of God. I am about to be honored and humbled at the manifestation of the Lord honoring His Word. I am about to enter into the divine presence of the Lord and the anointing of the Holy Spirit is about to acknowledge and empower me.

Knit Together in Love

Money cannot buy this; it is an honoring and acknowledgement of faith. My joy and faith are about to be increased. As we begin to have a deeper understanding of the "stand," and come together as a spirit-being community, knit together in love, the Impostor will lose tremendous ground on this Earth. This is God's plan for His people.

> *"That their hearts might be comforted, being knit together in love, and unto all riches of the full assurance of understanding, to the acknowledgement of the mystery of God, and of the Father, and of Christ;"*
> —Col: 2:2

Every time we stand with a brother or sister, our own faith increases. We grow together as the body of Christ, as it is meant to be. Our love and faith for each other will grow; our power as vessels of God will increase. This is not about one person speaking truth or preaching—this is about the new body of Christ, a community of an "Army of Healers," coming together, standing, in divine love for one another, making ourselves available to hold each other up in the battlefield. This action of community will enable us to receive the grace of God and our hearts will be opened by love.

The body of Christ must experience the personal healing that only comes from a step of faith in order to become empowered healers. The body must become a conscious body, a body in reality. Fear knows who's walking and who is declaring, and the Impostor's grip will not come under subjection with conversation or confessing alone. The anointing and power for healing comes with stepping out by faith and meeting Jesus the Healer. This is where the power of God is. It is embodied in a personal experience of laying down the idols of the Impostor's torment and illnesses. We do this with the faith in who we are—the righteousness of God in Christ. When we do this, we know and honor who He is, "The Great I Am," with all power given unto Him.

Section III: (Part II) Victorious Tales of Divine Retaliation

The "Christos-Sanity" of the Risen Spirit

We will come together as a body and joyfully strategize, pray, and plan miraculous healing days of "Divine Retaliation." I am talking about a new body, a conscious and evolved body, a mature body, one that is consecrated to transformation. Imagine a seasoned body that has individually taken back its land and thereby released the oppression of idols in its personal life. A resurrected spirit being who is living in the reality of "Christos-sanity," the sanity of the risen spirit. A body grounded by the experience of reclaiming its own personal territory by faith. This new body will not be a body focused on mortal flesh and victimization, nor a body following man—this is a sanctified body led by the Master. This is the refined body, the authentic people of a living God.

This new body will not focus on condemnation, sin and fornication.

This will be a body that speaks its truth with love and grows up in all aspects of Him. This will be a body that has evolved by faith, a body that deals in the moment, with the integrity of the spirit and an always righteous God. A body that has a spiritual focus.

> *"But speaking the truth in love, may grow up into him in all things, which is the head, [even] Christ:"*
> —Eph. 4:15

Your Holy Identity

Jane's Day of Kingdom Restoration

The day we planned for my sister Jane was a great day of healing. She arrived for her stand prepared with some of the foods to which she was highly allergic.

She had with her the feared McDonald burger, some French fries, and a Coke, the foods that were considered by the perceptions of mind control, to be a great show of faith. The Impostor had already set Jane up: *"You are eating what you have previously reacted to; you are demonstrating your faith."*

However, God does not see faith in doing just what you cannot do; God knows you have to up the ante on deception. The Holy Spirit, with its supreme wisdom, knows that you cannot make fear retreat on its own mortal, material territory. You have to "strike" it where it lives — there is a memory, a trauma, an unconscious belief, in the carnal mind, one that has to be shattered, "exorcised," and annihilated by the power of violent faith. This is the faith of the eternal immortal spirit. This is not mental ascent or a metaphysical concept, but violent faith, provoking the response of a living, active, participating God, a God that is always the fourth man in the fire.

> *"That your faith should not stand in the wisdom of men, but in the power of God."*
> —1 Cor. 2:5

If you are going to enter enemy territory, you will have to conquer the stronghold of fear by confronting the lie at the root. You are undoing what it has done to you.

Section III: (Part II) Victorious Tales of Divine Retaliation

> *"How can one enter into a strong man's house, and spoil his goods, except he first bind the strong man? And then he will spoil his house."*
> —Matt. 12:29

You Are the Tormentor

You have to break the stronghold, the inner belief; you are reversing trauma. You are now the one creating the trauma, the trigger, the anxiety. You are creating the mind jam—you are literally blowing the mind of fear. You have to be the aggressor. This battle is primal, territorial. You have to dominate.

I looked at Jane's arsenal of foods, and I remember thinking, *"No, Impostor, not on my watch, you are not taking my sister down."* I knew these food choices were a setup—there was not enough power in it. It was not a spiritual retaliation; it was an "attempt" of the flesh to get healed. Jane was totally sincere in her selection. This has nothing to do with good people or people who lack faith or people who have more faith. This is about deception. It is often hard to see yourself, to be subjective, when you are the one who is in the warfare. This is why standing with each other has so much power: there is a revelation in the stand, a revelation of "Divine Retaliation."

I said, *"Jane, that's great, you have made some good choices—you have done a wonderful job, and your faith is up; let's go to 7-Eleven and increase our warfare."* She had come this far, and she knew God was in it, she could feel it now. She was empowered to go a step further. She trusted the Christos in me. Jane's original batch of foods was the Impostor's selections. The Impostor knew she could eat those foods and "if" she didn't get the healing that she was expecting, she would get sick for a few days and recover. She would lose her hope for regaining those foods and lose more faith. She would then be victimized into doubt and taken out of the faith realm temporarily. Jane would be pushed back even more, she would be worse than where she was, she would be discouraged, depressed, hopeless, but alive to tell her tale of defeat.

Die to the Lie

In choosing the next food group, Jane would have to feel her selection could do permanent damage to her health. She would have to be told by her carnal mind, by its false belief, that the chosen foods could kill her. The Impostor would have its hidden, subconscious story provoked with the next group of foods. The voice of the Impostor may sound something like this: *"You will throw your whole body out of balance. You have suffered for years. Are you crazy? No one should eat that junk. These foods will create anaphylactic shock and a severe blood sugar reaction. The doctor told you that with your IBS, you should beware of certain food groups. You will surely destroy your digestive system; you are risking your internal organs. You have blood tests that show you have these diseases. This is real. You will never recover from this foolish display. What makes you think God is going to meet you? You have no facts to prove that idea."* We have all heard this voice, all doubt, fear, and anxiety—a prophetic mouthpiece for doom.

Section III: (Part II) Victorious Tales of Divine Retaliation

Fire

Jane would have to hear the Impostor's threats and oppose them. First, she would have to provoke error to speak. The voice of evil must be provoked to speak and reveal its veiled opinions. What did it really have? Not a hamburger... I knew exactly where my sister had to be to oppose fear and doubt, to oppose medical diagnosis. She had to lay her life down, or at least think she was. Only then would there be power. The flesh had to die on the frontline with Jesus. The spirit had to know Christ would be the fourth man in the fire. First, there had to be a fire, only a fire can mortify—this is not a flame that can scorch, but a refining fire.

What was the bottom line of the Impostor? What was the stronghold? What did it really have?

We walked into a 7-Eleven, where we purchased the feared beef jerky, Twinkies, some of their disgusting hot dogs, and cheap chocolates. We added food that, in all honesty, nobody should eat, let alone a person with an alleged digestive disorder. Jane's disorder, like everyone else's, had all the latest popular names, such as irritable bowel syndrome, and Epstein Barr Virus. She had also been diagnosed with ulcers, candidiasis and colitis.

We found some of the most inedible and utterly disgusting foods on the planet, and we purchased them. Evil was about to be provoked.

"That the trial of your faith, being much more precious than of gold that perisheth, though it be tried with fire, might be found unto praise and honour and glory at the appearing of Jesus Christ."
—1 Peter 1:7

Jane Ate

We went back to my house. And Jane ate; she simply ate. We sat down together at my kitchen table, and Jane ate. She ate all the disgusting, feared foods. Our plan was for her to stay over so I could join her for an additional disgusting, but Godly, breakfast.

Sometimes, there is an attack in the morning, the Impostor taking a last shot, for a comeback. Often, the Impostor can gain a little power in the unconscious carnal mind overnight. We were prepared. This is a very natural occurrence. The Impostor can be backed up for a moment and then re-group and try to return the next day. There is a possibility that the battle can continue for a few days. This often depends on how long the attack has been going on and how many battles have been conquered previously.

When facing the Impostor in your own life, if you are aware that the plot of the enemy is often to regroup, gain power, and strike again, it will not throw you off track. You will not relinquish your gain. You will just keep upping the ante. Each day, you will gain power, as you are wearing fear and deception down. Once you see fear bow to you, you become a confident warrior and enjoy the war. It is an exciting time—a time spent in the anointing and presence of God, an unforgettable and holy time.

This did not happen with Jane. The Impostor knew we would not buy it—that it could only relinquish more territory in an ongoing battle. Jane ate all the foods. Nothing happened. Not a stomach growl, not a burp. Nothing! All that occurred was joy and victory.

I Did Nothing

Notice, I did nothing, not a prayer, no casting out of fears, no adding of scripture. Nothing! I did not allow my flesh to take any credit or to exalt itself above the power of God. Jane ate. There were no teachings and no agenda— just eating. That was the necessary component. Her violent faith was demonstrated by her upping the ante, in her own personal "Divine Retaliation" and by her taking authority over her own mind by knowing and standing on her "divine rights." That in and of itself broke the stronghold of deception and fear. I did not need to add to it, only to be grateful to God and honor and respect faith. God would do it—she was in His fire, in His hands. What can anyone add to Jesus? How can we compete with the regenerative power of the Holy Ghost?

All the names of all the alleged diseases bowed to her faith. She got up the next morning, felt great, ate again, had some more junk food, and then went on her way to take her life and job back.

And she never had another food allergy attack again.

This is more powerful than any prayer, any deliverance prayer, any breaking of curses, any studying, reading, or reciting of scripture. This is "Righteousness Consciousness," a total reliance on the grace of God, knowing who you are and your divine rights.

A Revival of Righteousness

We are about to have a new spiritual healing revival on Earth, one that we have never seen before. It will be a completely unique impartation of divine power. This will not be accomplished by one exalted person with gifts of healing. Instead, it will be done by the body of Christ coming together knowing they are healed: a new body, standing together, a conscious body, a radically transformed body. One that is resurrected by claiming its divine rights, by violent faith and demonstration. When this happens, the world will change. God is about to raise our consciousness to His as we surrender who we are not.

An Army of Loving Healers

Every person of faith will have the power to heal others and change the world. There will be an army of healers, an army of love, total acceptance, joy, and bold power. Acceptance is Jesus; tolerance is the arrogance of the old nature. As this new conscious divine body becomes its true identity, the love of Christ will flow freely from these Holy Spirit filled spirit beings. The Church will become what it is supposed to be: the center of healing for all, the divine emergency room and the hospital for many. As we become our Holy Identity, these attributes will naturally restore us to our position of service and holiness on Earth. The Christos will be, all in all, without dogma. Religion will bow to spiritual connection and love. This is "The Perfect Law of Liberty."

When we pray from this place, we are praying from the Christos, from Christ Himself.

There is no law in love. There is no law in the fruits of the spirit. If there is no law, there are no traumas, no triggers, and no illness. Total freedom from the flesh.

Sin Consciousness will come under the subjection of Righteousness Consciousness. This is not about going to a church, or taking a class. This is about spiritual reality. This is about transforming and becoming who you are. This is the New Heaven on Earth. This is a new now, not just a moment, but a new move of God. A move of God, my brothers and sisters, that will bring the moment to you.

Chapter 35

Lily's Story of Confronting Demons

I will share another unique healing testimony of Divine Retaliation. This is Lily's Story, an interesting and small part of it. Lily had been coming to my deliverance groups in Los Angeles for about a year. She had experienced much healing and had gained a lot of spiritual authority, understanding, and empowerment.

Lily was a lovely lady of Chinese descent, in town from Toronto, and she had been staying with her family in the Arcadia area. Lily had decided to move in with roommates, closer to the city. It was there that she encountered her next Divine Retaliation healing opportunity.

She soon discovered in her new environment that she was unable to sleep at night. There were strange and intimidating sounds coming in through the walls.

Upon more closely examining her new surroundings, Lily discovered a design associated with Devil worship on the floor under her rug, right next to her bed. She had picked up the rug and found a symbolic, ritualistic painting of a pentagram, the six-pointed satanic star. This added to her anxiety, and soon after her finding it, she was unable to sleep at all. Lily began to investigate the person who had rented the room before her, and sure enough, she became aware of some bizarre stories of demonic events. This added to her concern and to the disturbance of her peace. She was now troubled by neck pain and backaches. She was attributing all of this to be from the demonic attacks in her new surroundings.

Lily was exhausted and confused. She did not know what to do, a lady of light and spiritual intent now living in a demonic environment. She initially wanted to bolt. However, her money and her commitment had been invested. Now what? Was she to never sleep again?

By the time I saw Lily a week later, she was traumatized, swollen, tired, and shaking. She shared her situation with our Los Angeles supportive deliverance group. As she spoke, I was immediately given a vision of the perfect retaliation, a revelation of what the Holy Spirit knew would undo the fear bow.

Usually when there is a healing vision, or a revelation of truth, I feel great joy, and I was feeling it. I was actually laughing out loud, not at her dilemma, but at the wonderful solution and empowerment that was to come. Healing was in the wings.

I think Lily did have some concerns, some doubts, about the power in the demonic realm.

I will share the exact warfare I invited Lily to execute. I suggested she go out and purchase some posters and images representing the Devil. I also asked her to find some demonic chants, the certifiable kind: horrifying sounds, evil chants and music, with growling vocals and a stomach-rattling bass.

Section III: (Part II) Victorious Tales of Divine Retaliation

The Warfare Plan of God

We devised a plan. Before Lily would go to bed, she would line her walls with large Devil-representing images, and then she would put on her Devil chants, with big speakers on high volume. She would then let the Impostor know that she had no fear of its Devil representing images, illusions, or any of its "self" created noise. She would tell the alleged demons she was on to the game. She would up the ante on demonic threats!

> *"Hey, Impostor, here are some well-known, and respected demonic activities for your pleasure. Impostor, goodbye and good night!"*

Bottom line, Impostor:

> *"There is no power but the power of God."*
> —Rom. 6:6

Lily Goes to Bed

Then, Lily went to bed. She kept her dialogue going with the Impostor. She watched all of its thoughts and threats. As Lily did this, she found a new power, as she expressed her authority, and, word-for-word, responded to threats of demonic attacks. She felt the fear mind bowing to her and her body being released. There is a God-given power to watch and have authority over intrusive fear thoughts, which is available in the actual battle. It is a perk of faith in action and your spirit will rise up in Righteousness Consciousness and be able to perform this battle in the moment. This may not happen on the practice field; it may not happen with scripture or your repeating affirmations with your church, or in your studies. However, when you have stepped out and are engaged in true combat with the Impostor, you are in the refining fire, and your flesh will feel the burn. Your violent faith will be honored, and you will experience the power of your Holy Identity.

Undoing the Bow

Needless to say, the ante was upped greater than the fear attack. Fear cannot stand if you are giving it more trauma than it is inflicting upon you. Lily conquered fear by demonstrating her faith in the supreme power of God; she let fear know that it had no power over her. She undid the bow. A very clear case of divine retaliation…

Perfect Peace

Lily was able to sleep in perfect peace that night and every night thereafter. For as long as she chose to remain in that environment, she had total comfort and joy. She also gained more power and more separation from the Impostor, with many other victimizing issues. Her faith had increased. She was no longer a swollen victim, afflicted with back and neck pain, considering an inconvenient move and a running away from the Impostor's illusion. Could I have done this for her with my Ph.D. in psychology? Could you have helped her with your expertise or advice?

Section III: (Part II) Victorious Tales of Divine Retaliation

If an entire church had prayed for Lily, would that have solved her problem? I am talking about the resurrection power of the Holy Spirit, grace by faith. I am speaking of the faith that is always there in every situation, for every person without exception, the law of faith, violent faith, simultaneously voluntarily laying down the idol and a radical reliance on Christ.

Chapter 36
Tommy's Story

I will share another healing accomplished with the power of the violent faith of Divine Retaliation.

Tommy had a great singing voice. He also had a "day job" and was very successful at it. He worked and lived in Los Angeles. His family was in the entertainment business and he had inherited much talent. He had also inherited generational alcoholism. After work, in the evenings, Tommy would head out to sing at a local karaoke bar.

There was a neighborhood bar that he frequented, where Tommy had become well-known. There was only one problem with his gift, and his nights out where he displayed it: he was usually drunk. Everyone saw him at his worst. He was the town's, or at least the bar's, favorite jovial alcoholic. He was well-known for his stumbling drunken repertoires.

Tommy had received a copy of my book, *Enforcing Grace*, from a client of mine who had been healed of chronic back pain and severe chemical sensitivities at one of my Los Angeles deliverance services.

Tommy was a person who was clearly predestined to take authority over his flesh with the divine healing process of retaliation. I believe that spiritual purpose is a powerful catalyst.

Tommy's History

Tommy came from a religious family, and his brother was a Christian minister. Tommy had always felt his brother had lost himself in religion. He shared with me that he had noticed his once fun-loving and very alive sibling had developed a diminished life force when he became involved in religious Christianity. He had become standoffish and repressed. This frightened Tommy and turned him off to organized Christianity. He was considered the spiritual black sheep of the family. However, after reading about retaliation and its healing power in *Enforcing Grace,* he contacted me and shared his history of years of alcoholism. As he spoke, I felt the presence of God. I knew that God was preparing him for service, and I was immediately led to facilitate in his Divine Retaliation.

Tommy was extremely intuitive, intelligent, and spiritually discerning. He was soon able to grasp the process of Divine Retaliation even better than I ever had. He was a natural warrior and had Godly imparted revelation.

He was ready, excited, and prepared to retaliate. I did not have to encourage him at all. There was only one question: what would his retaliation be? Where was his step of faith? What could he do to push fear back and intimidate the Impostor? How could a step of faith break the strongholds of Tommy's past? There was a past, of course, but it is irrelevant to the outcome of a spiritual retaliation. There is always a reason that someone becomes an alcoholic. There is always a mortal childhood reason for everyone's dysfunction and victimizing health conditions, a generational family predicament — a familiar spirit.

Section III: (Part II) Victorious Tales of Divine Retaliation

We discussed the who, what, where, and why of his drinking.

Tommy, who was extremely intelligent, successful, attractive, talented, and out every night, felt he was boring. Truth be known, he felt, without drinking and being buzzed, he could not even talk to people. He believed that he was not charming when sober and would never have the courage to sing. He would be rejected and lonely. That was the Impostor's claim and narrative. How do we up the ante on that? How do we back up "boring" by faith? Without drinking alcohol, Tommy would simply stay home alone, have no social life at all, and become depressed. How do we stop the desire to drink and then suddenly become charming and entertaining by faith? Tommy needed a miracle!

Backing Fear Up

The process of backing up fear is always the same. We do more of what the Impostor is afraid to do. Tommy was willing to do anything. He grasped the premise and there was nothing that could hold him back. Tommy was able and excited to gain territory. He had ample faith for any opposing action.

The Warfare Plan

God had a plan. I have noticed God's plan is always totally rational yet simultaneously bizarre.

Tommy was led to back the Impostor's fear threats up, by going out even more. Instead of staying home in isolation, he was to go out every night! God commanded that he continue to enjoy his nightlife. Tommy was to add more bars and more karaoke places at which to sing.

He was to confront his fear and keep going out—more outings, more singing, more bars, but without the booze. Sounds bizarre! Instead of going to one bar, he was to add five bars and sing at them all: every night.

I had the privilege of watching what occurred. I lived nearby, so I joined Tommy in his pursuit of sober karaoke. I was invited by God and Tommy to stand with him.

The Decision

The minute the decision of faith was made, Tommy's countenance changed. His spirit became excited to live in freedom, and to no longer be oppressed by alcohol. It was a spiritual decision—a decision of faith, not an exercise of self-will or a decision to try and stop drinking. He trusted in the power of God, and up in the spirit he went. His Christos rose to the occasion.

Tommy understood the premise. He was a spirit being, and God would meet him by faith; he just had to keep moving...

A Miracle Healing

It was a profound miracle. He went from place to place talking, singing, and connecting to everyone. Within a week, with a little wearing down of the Impostor, Tommy was freely giving his testimony. The power of his testimony was very strong, as everyone had known him as a drunk for nearly twenty years. When Tommy was seen as a light, it was very large. An incredible testimony, his being out living large in bars, singing, dancing, and laughing completely sober was incredible to the onlooker. People would see us together and come up to me and inquire, *"What did you do, Rev. Juliana?"* they would ask. My simple response: *"Nothing—what could I do?"* I never even prayed for him. What could anyone do? Tommy made a decision by faith and upped the ante on fear. He has never felt a need to drink again. He has a beautiful testimony and has helped many people gain their freedom from alcohol. One less egg to fry…generational alcoholism.

There Is Always a Root

It is easy to judge a miracle healing and say, *"Well, he didn't get to the root; he had psychological problems and they will return."* There was, of course, a root: Tommy's alcoholic mother left his father and her four children when he was ten. He was the oldest child, his dad worked long hours in the entertainment business, away a lot on movie locations. Tommy was often left with the responsibility of taking care of his siblings. He learned at an early age to take care of the house cleaning, cooking and other people, but not himself.

Tommy also had guilt feelings about his mother leaving the entire family when he was ten years of age. He had always felt he had something to do with her decision to leave his father. As he started to live as the spirit person in his Holy Identity, Tommy's self-esteem increased. Without drinking, he was better able to take care of himself.

Tommy had gained clarity by faith and the ability to sort out his thoughts and not receive the old guilt-ridden and condemning thoughts of the past. After a short while, he was able to let go of his unhappy past and live a spiritual life of empowerment. Tommy began to live outside of his misery, outside of his old self. He even reconciled with his mother and now has a great and loving relationship with her.

Instead of being a codependent caretaker of the flesh, being a nice guy, and going along with others for their approval solely to please them, he became a truth speaker and a light giver. He was in spiritual service, and an edifier of the purposes of God.

Cut to the Chase

As a woman who was a psychologist in one of the largest cities in the world for many years, I am delighted to say that Divine Retaliation may be primal, but it is still the all-encompassing short cut to our physical health, mental peace, and emotional well-being. It cuts to the chase of spiritual transformation; it is the spirit being elevated above the mind, where it is supposed to be in our natural God-given position of authority. It has the power to harmonize the spirit-mind-heart and body for all human beings living on this planet; it is dominion on Earth.

> *"But we all, with open face beholding as in a glass the glory of the Lord, are changed into the same image from glory to glory, even as by the Spirit of the Lord."*
> —2 Cor. 3:18

Bringing the Flesh under Subjection

Taking territory decreases the power of the flesh. If you take enough territory, you will be living the spirit person's life, no matter what your past history and physical conditions may have been. You will overcome it all. Staying in the fire with Jesus is the safest and most empowering place to be on Earth. It is the shortcut. The fire is where you take your step of faith, where you oppose the fears and deceptions of the Impostor's lying egocentric mind. This is the key to healing, the key to our faith walk.

The Voice of Faith

Faith says, *"Take something from me, and you will pay. It will cost you. You take something from me, you will lose. I am your master. I will teach and train you to obey me, to come under the authority of the will of God."* (Enforcing Grace, p. 274)

Going into the fire with Jesus, where He will be the fourth man in your situation, is simply planning a little spiritual warfare.

"Lo, I see four men loose, walking in the midst of the fire, and they have no hurt; and the form of the fourth is like the Son of God."
—Dan. 3:23

Remember, if you can do it yourself, you do not need the help of Christ.

When you surrender your ability to overcome an obstacle, let go of worldly help, and recognize the impossibility of your situation, you become more willing to up the ante and add a little more challenge. Only then when you fully acknowledge that there is no doubt about it, you cannot without the power of God accomplish this task, get yourself healed, or fix your problem, you will experience "divine intervention."

This is the promise of Divine Retaliation: you have given it to God. You are simply not able—it is a total surrender to faith. It is the essence of Righteousness Consciousness. This is how we apprehend our spiritual authority on Earth. There is no other way to get it and no other path offers it. Sometimes people get there by hitting rock bottom. Sometimes we are so desperate for a miracle that we become willing to radically rely on God.

Without taking territory back from the Impostor, it is impossible to maintain your Holy Identity. It is not a one-time experience. It is the lifestyle of a warrior, a spirit consecrated to be a conqueror of fear and deception. This is another reason why the works of the flesh have to be eliminated, as they are the Impostor's distraction to your gaining any additional power over it.

I had to hit my rock bottom, in my own personal experience. I had nowhere to go and no other option but Jesus. You do not have to reach the depths of despair, get sick, or go insane. Once you become aware and choose to be proactive in your territory, you can always choose to enlarge and expand your spirit in taking more territory, and there is always more territory to take.

There Is Always More Power to Appropriate

If you ever feel powerless, if you need strength or an elevation of your spirit, maybe you don't know exactly what happened, but you are oppressed... If you are feeling a little lowered, sensitive, or weak, take some land. Make fear retreat.

Section III: (Part II) Victorious Tales of Divine Retaliation

Take Some Power Back

It does not even have to be in the same area where you may have relinquished power, as power is power. You can heal your bad back by regaining your power from another deception. My back was healed when I put all the alleged toxic feared mercury fillings back in my mouth by faith—more faith, more victory, more power.

I had a client who was experiencing sudden hearing loss and going deaf, and I did not have the root of the issue—I simply did not know. We did know some other areas where she had given up power, and when she confronted and conquered those areas, she gained power. Her hearing came back 100 percent. We were amazed. Any re-acquisition of land relinquished is a step to regain power in your life. The key is to take what is stopping you from moving ahead. Take what is taking you.

Always More Land to Conquer

I have not run out of fear to conquer. I am still here on Earth, and if you are reading this book, so are you. I have recently laid down my eyeglasses, and I am able to see and drive without them, seeing better at night without them, than I was with the glasses. I am in the process of seeing perfectly, with divine eyesight, my God-given right. I was led to see imperfect vision as just another fear block, another belief of the Impostor. God made it easy for me, as I could not get a prescription that enabled me to see well. I had to re-think. I had not identified it as an idol. I had gone totally unconscious in my pursuit to see better and became dependent on glasses. I started to become afraid to drive at night. When I finally saw it, I knew I had bowed to glasses, years of glasses, and I knew I had to stop the bow to have my vision restored. I ultimately received so much more than improved vision. I began to have better eye contact with others, see brighter colors, and have a new relationship with nature. I started to "see" and appreciate flowers, grass, and trees.

The divine eye connects with all of God's creations and feels love in doing so, as the divine eye is connected to the heart. I began to "see" differently, as true seeing slows us down, since it is in the moment. It is the heart feeling and connecting through the eyes, the windows of the soul. I am now only wearing glasses to work on the computer, but this too will eventually be corrected, and more blessings will come. I am free to buy any reading glasses at CVS or elsewhere, not trying to find a "better optometrist" or the perfect glasses to improve my ability to see. I "saw" it for what it was. One more Sin Consciousness belief, attempting to tell me my vision was less than perfect. The important thing for you to remember is not to buy into the lie of the Impostor telling you that are your physical body and it is your master, your God, and that you must listen to and obey its threats.

Chapter 37
Leslie's Story

Leslie was a disciple of mine who had gained much personal healing and wisdom in the years that she had been serving in my Los Angeles ministry. Leslie had a unique and amazing gift of casting mental illness right out of the human mortal mind. I had the pleasure of encountering many traumatized and mentally ill individuals, return the next day, after her precious ministry, declaring their clarity.

One tormented soul, whom I will never forget returned the next day, after she had prayed for him and said, *"This is the first time I can think without voices talking over the thoughts in my head. This is the first day of my life that I am without mental torment."*

She was a very gifted healer, and God used her in many diverse areas. She served in a downtown LA skid row ministry, where she prayed for and fed the homeless. She was also attending college, and she was working as a waitress in a restaurant in the San Fernando Valley at night.

She had worked in this restaurant for many years. Suddenly, they decided to add an outdoor patio, one for smokers. This is where the opportunity for spiritual promotion became available.

Your Holy Identity

Leslie's Opportunity Strikes

Leslie had developed a terrible cough and a throat infection. She could no longer serve food in the patio area where the smokers dined, as the Impostor informed her that she had developed an allergy to smoke. Soon after that hostile suggestion, Leslie had become so sensitive to smoke that, even when she was inside the restaurant, she was hyper-aware of the outside smoke and coughed continuously.

The Impostor labeled her condition as bronchitis. Her doctor agreed and after a round of antibiotics, her situation worsened.

I received her call at 9:30 P.M. She was distraught, saying, "I have to quit my job. I can no longer work here. My health is at stake."

Who she was in her Holy Identity, of course, knew better. But the Impostor had worn her down. It does this with medical diagnosis and medication. This was a moment of truth for my sister, a challenge to rid herself of any hidden fears, any doubts of the fullness of God's complete transformational redemption and her own healing and divine rights to be healed. She was being led by God, to take a stand. The Impostor loves to create blind spots in us all.

I instantly remembered, when I first came down from my environmentally safe mountaintop location in Santa Barbara, I often felt fearful when I had to re-enter the world. The world of car fumes, cigarettes, and airplane fumes still intimidated me. I gave my sister the exact retaliation that God had given me regarding smoke fumes.

By this time, Leslie was coughing so hard she could hardly hold a conversation. "How will I support myself?" Leslie continued, "This is a great job, it suits my life, and it is near my home. I like and know everyone here and the pay and tips are great. I can even take time out and run home to walk my dog."

I responded, "You do not have to quit this job until you are ready to. Do not allow the Impostor to inconvenience you. It is a bluff. Call it."

Leslie remained distraught, saying, *"How do I call the bluff of Marlboros?"*

God's Warfare Plan

"How do I up the ante on cigarettes?" Leslie said, confused. *"Go and buy some cigars,"* I said. *"Smoke a nice big Tiparillo cigar all night tonight."* She got it. She immediately felt the presence of God and heard the power of the spirit in my suggestion.

Leslie did just that. She purchased the cigars, called me back, and we both laughed in utter joy. She lit up in her tiny car, a small space with a lot of smoke. This was her car, not an outdoor patio, but an enclosed vehicle, with no air, no escape. The cough, the lying symptoms of the alleged bronchitis, disappeared faster than it had arrived. The healing was instantaneous.

This Divine Retaliation worked the same way all retaliations do.

The Impostor had my sister backed up with a "fear of" smoke. The threat was she would have to quit her job or ruin her health. These were her only options—lose your job or lose your health.

There was nothing wrong with Leslie's lungs. They had just become constricted by fear and by the belief that she had developed an allergic reaction and had bronchitis—no more, no less. It could have been a constriction due to an emotional reason—I am not negating that. Let us assume her lungs had become constricted in the fear of losing her husband, her job, or a fear of being fired. The confrontation of fear does not have to be related to the issue. It just has to be bigger than the presented fear of the body, larger than the threat of the Impostor.

Dominion is dominion and fear must bow to your divine rights. If you are about to lose a job or a relationship, being ill is not going to help you. It is the Impostor kicking you when you are down. I assure you after you take your power back, with a few Divine Retaliations, your solutions will be very easy to perceive. You will be higher than the emotional problems that the Impostor has created.

Beloved, fight for what you want, your heart's desires and spiritual purposes. Do not allow the Impostor to ambush you and arrest you from moving ahead. Fight with eternal wisdom and faith.

I have seen wonderful, kind, and authentic believers with great hearts and faith beaten down and blamed for attacks of cancer, being accused of unforgiveness and other unkind interpretations of their identity. This malicious verbal abuse comes from a spirit of condemnation, an unholy attack on God's people.

One does not get cancer due to unforgiveness—symptoms of cancer are due both to an identity conflict and a bow to someone, something, or the Impostor itself. It is usually from a severe disempowerment or a victimization. I have found cancer and lupus and most diseases are mostly rooted in codependency, where the afflicted bows to the needs of others and does not take care of themselves.

A failure to be true to oneself, a compromise of one's own desires and integrity are often at the root of illness. A generational belief that you are here exclusively to take care of others, and a going along passively and silently negating your own heart's desires, can create body pain and illness. This behavior stems from a limited self-worth in the old nature. Cancer, like most illnesses, is an integrity issue, an issue of the heart. It has very little to do with forgiveness or unforgiveness. That idea is too often the hateful accusation and second punch of the merciless attitude of Sin Consciousness. Forgiveness is not a mortal process; it is a characteristic of the spirit.

There is nothing wrong with you, beloved. Do not allow the mortal mind of man to make you wrong. This is not Christ. This is the personification of a counterfeit consciousness. This is exactly what the Lord is changing. We are living in a wonderful time, my family. You will live and partake in the new "now" healing time on God's Earth. We will stand together. We will enter the sanctity of identity discrepancy and no longer receive the accusations and erroneous interpretations of the Impostor. No one can do it alone. It is meant to be done in unity. My faith is in you and with you to rise up and allow us to be graciously knit together in the power of divine love.

Chapter 38
Jacob's Story

I met Jacob at an animal shelter in West Los Angeles. We shared our love for animals and shared our hearts; we had become fast friends in between cage cleaning, adoption events, and dog walking. Eventually, Jacob adopted Pita, a lovely Siamese kitten. He was thrilled with her. She talked, cuddled, and was his constant companion.

Jacob and I normally worked in the dog section, but Pita had been brought in one day and he saw her in the waiting room, and they had an instant connection. He fell in love with her, adopted her, and took the little doll home with him.

After a few weeks, Jacob came into the shelter one morning with a huge rash, a rash that covered his entire body.

A Medical Diagnosis

He was crying. *"I have to give Pita up,"* he said. *"I was taken to the emergency room last night, with a painful rash and covered with hives. They discovered I have an allergy to cats. They tested me and I have a severe reaction to cat dander. I don't know what to do... Pita is staying with my neighbor, and I cannot go near her. She is crying and upset, and my heart is broken. I have not slept, and the medication they gave me is making me confused and groggy."*

I invited Jacob to come and stay with me at my house that evening. We prayed, he got some rest and I shared my personal healing of allergies with him. Jacob was a gay, Jewish man, someone that did not have any experience with spiritual healing. I explained he that did not have to give up Pita, that it was an absurd idea.

The Battlefield

We had to go to the battlefield. I knew Jacob did not have any allergies to animals but had only absolute divine love and compassion for them. I had a sense that something else had triggered his reactions. I inquired what else had happened in the last twenty-four hours that may have created some stress. *"Nothing,"* he said. He went home from work, Pita greeted him, he fed her, and then his mom called from Florida. *"How is she doing?"* I inquired. Jacob informed me that she was not doing well and wanted to come back to Los Angeles.

There is always a reason, my friends, for your physical manifestations and symptoms, just not the one the Impostor is presenting. There is always a revelation in your symptoms: a connection to be made, an awareness to gain. The Impostor is in darkness and denial. It is looking for an opportunity to overcome you and weaken you by taking your heart's desires. It wants to point the finger of blame outside of your control, blaming Devils, rashes, cats, body parts, and illnesses.

The fear of his mom returning to live with him, or close to him, sent Jacob into unconscious repressed fear and anger. He finally had peace in his life, and she was returning.

Repression

The repressed fear and anger that the Impostor was reticent in allowing Jacob to acknowledge manifested in a rash. This was rooted in the fear of his not taking care of himself with his mom and falling into his old patterns of fear, oppression, and guilt, and then bowing to her demands. These repressed emotions emerged as a rash covering his entire body. I did not go into all of this with him at the time—that would come later, after the healing, with the luxury of emotional peace and confidence.

The root of the symptom is irrelevant to the authority of the spirit in healing. This is the vital point that this story makes abundantly clear.

There are two parts to a healing. One is spiritual: you have a divine right to be healed by the grace of God. You have a divine right to appropriate your healing by faith.

You also have a transformational process to grow in, mature in, and to have your consciousness raised to your Holy Identity by acknowledging deception and correcting it.

There is a commitment to God to be focused and purposed on your path, consecrated to guard your heart, to be true to yourself, and ultimately to grow in your power, authenticity, and integrity.

The first part of Righteousness Consciousness is spiritual integrity, and your divine rights; the second is emotional integrity, the honoring of the issues in your heart and taking care of yourself therein.

Jacob would have time to deal with his conflict with his mom and grow in that area, with the luxury of divine health, when he was clear, medication-free, and with his beloved Pita at his side.

My heart broke for my dear friend and for Pita. I could not bear to think that she was crying for him, her life disrupted by fear and uncertainty about losing her Jacob, and her wondering where she would end up. I don't know about you, but animals get to me.

God Had a Plan

We would use Jacob's spiritual authority to bring the body and the rash under subjection, with the supreme power of Divine Retaliation.

Jacob had a divine right to be healed. He was a precious human being on this Earth, a child of the living God.

He loved Pita and was not going to let her go without a fight. His love had faith in it. Faith worketh by love...

Jacob's Comeback

I was led to ask one of the other volunteers if she could switch places with Jacob for the next day—she worked on the cat side. I explained that Jacob needed some training time with the cats. There were about fifty cats currently in the shelter. Yes, fifty, not one little Pita girl, but fifty, in all sizes, shapes, ages, and colors. *Yes, Impostor fifty cats! What you got?* Fifty hairy, smelly, big and small cats to jump on Jacob. I am laughing now

Section III: (Part II) Victorious Tales of Divine Retaliation

in the memory of it. It was quite the scene. Well, by now, you can likely surmise what happened: absolutely nothing. Jacob spent two days on the cat side and was allergy, rash, symptom, and medication-free. He called the Impostor's bluff by upping the ante on deception and fear.

God Met Jacob Exactly Where He Was

God met him there. Jacob did not have a lot of knowledge with which to go to war. He had hope—"hope" to win his Pita back. He confronted his fear. He had heart. In the eyes of God, Jacob's heart was sacred. His heart spoke volumes, more than a lot of vain repetition of empty words prayed or warfare without corresponding action.

He picked up his beloved Pita on the second night, and they have been living happily together ever since. As a matter of fact, Jacob eventually got a second cat to keep Pita company when he was at work. He also gained significant spiritual wisdom, trust, and a relationship with a loving God. He began to understand how he could be triggered by a phone call and how not expressing himself in the moment could affect his health.

Jacob's transformation had begun, and he committed to be true to himself. He was now in alignment with his spiritual purpose and has a valuable respect and gratitude for his true nature.

Jacob's Root

The root of Jacob's allergic reactions was eventually conquered by his becoming aware of and making the heart, mind, spirit, body connection. He did not have to suffer with debilitating symptoms for years, on toxic medications, unconscious with rashes, and without pets to comfort him, in order to gain divine consciousness. He did not have to live in repressed anger to receive healing. That is never God's plan. God has already healed you. Taking back what God has freely given you, in a complete and total redemption, is always God's plan. Jacob simply and innocently honored it.

The Cosmic Joke

As you are beginning to perceive the truth in some of these testimonies, you are beginning to comprehend, that the Impostor's presented problem is rarely the issue. It is the fear and repression of reality being created by the triggers and misleading physical symptoms of the Impostor. These manifestations ultimately have very little to do with the body.

When we are standing against these deceptions, we have to win. They do not even exist. That is the cosmic joke of the literal "matter"—they do not even exist. That is the bitter sweetness of the entire stand. Like all of these precious folks demonstrating their holy and violent faith, when God was healing me, I truly believed that I was laying my life down, that I could die... I truly believed I was risking my health and my body. However, as I have become seasoned in the battlefield of God's refining fire, I have learned that most of these alleged illnesses do not even exist. They truly do not. I am not speaking metaphysically, but literally. There is no such thing as allergies, lupus, etc. There are only manifestations of fear, doubt, repressed emotions, triggers of the past, and illusions of our material physicality, and mortality. They are manifestations

Section III: (Part II) Victorious Tales of Divine Retaliation

of the Impostor's ego carnal mind exalting itself above your Holy Identity.

Jacob would never again react to cat dander, to which he had never actually reacted to begin with. However, if he would have continued to repress his emotions, Jacob would have many more symptoms of compromise in the future. Had he not made the connection between his heart, mind, and body, and if he did not confront or acknowledge how he truly felt about his mom and their unresolved circumstances, the triggers could be evoked again and demand his attention, they would go on to create pain, rashes, and other discomforts. They might even create havoc with similar personalities that might remind him of her behavior.

Most of our health issues are based in these triggers from the past. Divine Retaliation eliminates and brings to the light, the denial of our hidden trauma. We can then respond freely and with confidence and clarity, and begin to deal real.

I have found after a retaliation that the real issues will emerge organically, through revelation, without symptom subterfuge.

Chapter 39
Charlene's Story

Charlene was one of my dearest friends from my environmentally ill past, my pre-Christ home girl. We had been best phone friends when I was too sick and too chemically sensitive to leave my house, when I was still stuck in isolation in the mountains of Santa Barbara. Charlene, at that time, had been living in total isolation in a trailer in the hills of Tucson. She had been diagnosed with multiple chemical sensitivities, immune system dysfunction, and thyroid disease. We were both unable to leave our homes at that time and we were very grateful to have each other to commiserate with.

Since then, Charlene had experienced much healing and was out of her trailer—she was living in an apartment in LA and able to eat and digest food. She had been attending one of my deliverance groups in Los Angeles, on and off for a year. However, she was still hypersensitive to the energy of certain people. The doctors called this "Electric Magnetic Sensitivity."

Trauma Triggers

The Lord interpreted her situation differently, on a deeper, more holistic and comprehensive level, and had shared with me the details of what was happening to disrupt her moving ahead.

Charlene's problems had nothing at all to do with an electromagnetic or energetic sensitivity, as they were actually based on triggers from her past, shutting her heart down in the new moment. The Impostor's narrative and distracting claim was that these manifestations were a heightened sensitivity to the energy of other people, or an electromagnetic-based dilemma. Religion has the devil, and the medical community has its own distracting rational diagnosis and self-justifications.

What was actually happening on an emotional, psychological, and spiritual level was much more complicated. She was being re-stimulated by the old creature's fears of her abusive childhood. Certain people, sometimes aggressive or louder folk, would, on a subconscious level, trigger her memory bank and remind her of someone from her unpleasant past.

Perhaps this was a memory of a time she was unable to take care of herself in victimizing situations. There had been a lot of verbal and even physical abuse—this is often referred to as trauma and it is indeed traumatic. It is not an easy condition to cure, as we can observe from many of our precious and emotionally disturbed veterans as they return from war, disabled by trauma. I knew what had to happen, yet I was not sure how I could create the atmosphere that she needed. We needed a group of very loud, aggressive people, folks with a very active, vibrant and bold outgoing energy. We had to find a way to up the ante on the Impostor's fear of past traumas and fear of aggression. We needed to freak the Impostor out, disrupt its memories—"memories" held deep in the old nature's mortal, unconscious fear memory bank.

Charlene had to show the Impostor's fear memory and its "fear of" interpretations that she was no longer intimidated by them. She had to be willing to go into the fire with Jesus and a lot of aggression. She needed more aggression than she felt triggered by when she had a fear reaction…a lot more.

The Bigger Horse

The Divine Retaliation premise is always the same. It gets bigger than the fear, a very basic primal attack back. Charlene was currently living alone in a small place, no roommates, no pets, with very little social activity. Her connections were limited by the Impostor's fear triggers.

I was living in a big house in Woodland Hills, California, at the time, where I had my house church and held my healing services. I was led by the Holy Spirit to do a retaliation weekend from my home. The retaliation was to be a weekend party with a lot of loud, expressive, and aggressive folks. Aggressive, loud, outgoing, and bold people are not hard to come by in Los Angeles. We had everyone from our healing group bring their loudest friends. This was a weekend jam, a stay-over, and there were aggressive people all over the house. They were in sleeping bags, on couches, talking, babbling, singing, sharing their hearts boldly with gusto, with noise, with instruments.

There was no place to hide, to escape, for the hypersensitive. That weekend, the rooms in my house were as energetically intense as they could possible be! For an energetically sensitive person, this was make it or break it. This could be heaven, or this could be hell for Charlene!

The fear that Charlene was experiencing had been keeping her from getting close to other people, thus, keeping her connections limited. This, to her, was a life-threatening event. The Impostor will always go for your connections. In the Kingdom of God, and in life, perfect love casts out fear. The Impostor is very resistant to being evicted!

The more we are able to get out of the Impostor's problem-focused mentality, the more space we have for love. We are able, through connection, to take the pressure, and worry of the ego fear mind off the heart in the moment. The heart is created to and naturally opens in divine love. It is who we are. This can be easily done with authentic connections, but not if we are reacting to them, by being constantly pushed back by fear triggers to relinquish our friends or pay the price of mental suffering and body pain.

Laying the Idol Down

Charlene had been unconsciously bowing to the fear trigger limitations of the carnal mind. Charlene was not doing this deliberately. She was walking out her transformation led by the spirit. No one bows to the Impostor consciously—it is not possible. This was her next surrender, her next idol to lay down, to be able to grow in her Holy Identity.

Charlene was no longer a fearful victimized mortal seed. She was a woman of God, with all the fruits of the spirit. She was in the process of activating her identity by violent faith. She agreed to partake in the retaliation weekend. She was not quite sure how it would work, but she felt led to take it on.

Section III: (Part II) Victorious Tales of Divine Retaliation

A New Day

By the second day, Charlene had stepped into her Holy Identity and she had nothing but divine love for everyone who had attended, from the loudest to the biggest, the boldest, and the most aggressive, a far cry from being triggered. What happened?

Where did the hypersensitivity go?

The Human Heart

I believe two things occurred simultaneously. One unexpected perk that we could not have foreseen was that her heart had been for so long deprived of human connections it had shut down in despair. Charlene had so wanted to be close to other human beings, but every time she would get close to someone, join a group, or start a new friendship, a fear trigger would grip her heart, and she would have to relinquish the new territory. In her situation, the territory was connections. The human entitlement to connection, to fellowship, had become a deep unfulfilled desire.

When Charlene's heart saw it could have this—not just her foods back, but people, all kinds of people, any kind of person without any concerns, with no reactions, no price to pay, that she could truly be back in the human race, *sans* "old-self"-imposed limitations—it simply opened. When Charlene's heart achieved its bottom-line desire, connections with people, it just released and surrendered. And what was in her heart, when it opened, is exactly what is in yours: divine love.

Perfect love casts out fear. Perfect love is much larger than all our fear triggers. It is, after all, perfect and divinely powerful. All the triggers, the traumas of the past, bowed to her faith and the fruit of her divine love. My only regret was that I do not have it all on video. It was a magnificent sight to behold—the party of all parties—a love festival.

The Power of Love

Love was in the air. After the fear of the energy of aggression and intimidation was confronted, Charlene's life changed. She became aware how much she needed other people and how much she loved them and changed her lifestyle accordingly. She realized that when she became sensitive to energy, she just needed to get around more people, not run from them, but embrace them. Charlene needed to consciously choose to add to her human collection of friends and connections. She chose to open up to and embrace a diverse population of people. She opened up to folks from all walks of life and became a walking ministry of divine love.

Finally, Charlene moved in with other ladies, got a puppy, and is now dating without fear of trigger repercussions. A free spirit! She is full of love and gratitude and a profound blessing to be around.

The Perks of Divine Retaliation

I am always amazed at the perks of a Divine Retaliation and the things I am unable to predict that will be added to a healing. God's perfect prophetic insights are so much greater than our psychological understanding or the shallow and limiting works of religion.

Section III: (Part II) Victorious Tales of Divine Retaliation

I do not think I have ever seen a transformation as grand as Charlene's. Her short story and retaliation healing are really the essence of all our issues. Her victory was magnified by violent faith. In just one spirit-led weekend, she was able to open the door for all of us to grasp the simplicity and beauty of God's plan.

This was very different from an "electromagnetic sensitivity" diagnosis, and the medical hypothesis and conclusion, which was to live in isolation and avoid all chemicals, people, electrical stimuli, and other alleged allergens. That turned out to be the very opposite of what she needed to heal.

In Christ, we confront our fears in perfect love and authority. The more we are deceived into bowing to the convoluted mentality of the Impostor, the more we become seduced into letting go of our God-given divine rights and authority. We then inevitably become victims of the Impostor's fear mind and shrink in our power and life force.

If we do this enough, we become sick and depleted, not from illness, but from the undiagnosed bow.

Chapter 40

Kathleen's Story

Kathleen was a chiropractor and natural health practitioner by occupation and also a strong lifelong believer in Christ. She was an extremely sensitive woman, and with her many gifts of the spirit and prolific discernment, she had helped and healed many people.

She also had many sensitivities of her own, as many healers and caretakers do. Kathleen was very interested in learning the deliverance ministry, and we had become instant good buddies and close sisters in the Lord.

She enjoyed the depth of comprehending the root of symptoms of illness and disharmony, and how they could manifest in the body, and was learning about it her own. Kathleen had been suffering for years, with multiple food allergies and other sensitivities, and, of course, she had her own emotional and generationally inherited triggers.

Letting It Go

Like many advanced spiritual folks, healers, caretakers, and especially Christians, Kathleen had a belief that, letting everything go was somehow desirable and humble.

Letting everything go is not humility—it is the Impostor creating darkness and denial and destroying your body with repressed rage and anger.

Kathleen was learning that her symptoms would worsen when she did not express herself. Her new mantra became, *"I do not let things go—I express my heart in the moment."*

Repressed Anger

By identifying and making the connection of her reticence and her symptoms, she soon became able to stop her chronic and painful physical reactions completely. As Kathleen stopped bowing to a generationally inherited "niceness" agenda, she simultaneously became true to the integrity of her heart. She was learning to not receive the condemnation mentality of the Impostor. The Impostor feels it has a right to punish us for the old creature's compromises and it does this by creating repressed emotions.

It has no legal right to do this, and as Kathleen became cognizant of her divine rights, she was able to receive grace. Even if she missed a moment, a situation, or an expression, she would not have to suffer the consequences. Redemption is now, in this moment, not just for the afterlife. In Heaven, you will not have the issues of the flesh.

Sometimes when repression has been a way of life for a while, a generationally inherited way of responding to situations, the Impostor has to be pushed back from the liberty it has gained. It needs to be re-trained to come under the subjugation of the spirit or it will defer to the self-defending self-exaltation of the flesh. It has its own default system. When it feels your heart is unguarded, it defaults to rage, which is a mortal self-protection mechanism.

The old creature can manifest a lot of over-reactions and unconscious fears and shut down your life force, compounding your problem with a flesh gone wild in a self-exaltation effort to defend who you are not.

I believe this is where the "let everything go" belief originates: a sincere effort to arrest self-exaltation, but in an unholy way. God's way is to deal real, speak your truth with humility and love, to resolve a situation, which is a win-win, not an avoid-avoid. Avoidance is not a fruit of the spirit—it is a bow and a compromise of your integrity. We want to default to our spiritual fruits.

The Arrogance of Desensitization

The Impostor can deceive us into thinking we are being humble. However, desensitizing oneself to our reality and to other people, can also be the height of arrogance.

The Path to Mental Illness

The Impostor, as you know by now, wants to turn everything into an idol adding adventure and create a bow. Denial is not a spiritual fruit. It is the path to mental illness, not Christ. Kathleen was a fast learner, had a lot of faith, and had quickly taken back all her foods that had given her alleged allergic reactions. And soon she was able to eat anything she desired.

She took her voice back in all her relationships. Kathleen became more authentic in her marriage. She began to express her beautiful heart to her husband and her back pain and emotional well-being were restored.

She had one more area of her life where she was still not free. This brings us to Kathleen's Divine Retaliation.

Kathleen's Retaliation

Jewelry! She could not wear jewelry without blowing up like a balloon and getting severe reactions: coughing, crying, itching. Anytime Kathleen put gold, silver, or any metal on her body, she would swell up like a balloon, cry, and be intimidated by pain and fear to remove it rapidly.

She could not even wear her own wedding ring. We developed a Godly Divine Retaliation to resolve this last interference in my sister's peace. The Impostor did not want her to be free. It had this last issue, and knew with just one deception, it could expand its territory and create lying symptoms in the future.

I was led to make this a group experience. I was confident the Impostor would bow immediately—a group experience of healing increases everyone's faith who is there, including my own.

Kathleen brought in all the jewelry that she had ever reacted to in her adult life. She had a drawer full of old necklaces, bracelets and rings. The entire group collected every piece of jewelry we had stored in our homes! We decorated Kathleen with jewels from head to toe. The Impostor was completely overwhelmed, years of reactions for naught. Kathleen looked like a bejeweled Maharaja, or at least Mr. T. Not a peep from the opposition. It was much more than the Impostor could ever anticipate. We used every kind of jewel— it was like taking candy from a baby, gold and silver anyway.

The Impostor surrendered without a battle; there were too many of us and we had no intention of bowing. The Impostor is able to identify the fear level of the environment, and if it discerns violent faith, it will give up rapidly. That does not mean it will not bow if you have to put more time into it.

I have been in battles for days. In that instance, it is always good to let the Impostor know you are fighting to win. *"Impostor, I don't care how long it takes, I am here for the victory; I will see you bow."* Sometimes, just declaring that is enough to break its hold. In Kathleen's situation, she was never troubled by any metal again. Her husband bought her a beautiful necklace as a victory gift and gave it to her at the next meeting— sweet, sweet victory.

What happened? The law of faith conquered years of torment in a few minutes. It did so without any casting out of evil, without prayer or drama. Pain, itching and despair were conquered by Kathleen's own decision of faith and her action of opposing deception by upping the anti with violent faith.

Chapter 41

Mike's Story

I am going to tell Mike's story. It is a story about an injury from an accident. Mike's problem was different as it was not an ongoing circumstance, not chronic pain, but a then-current and active injury.

Mike was a healthy man, an athlete, in perfect shape before he got rear-ended in an auto accident. The Impostor always has a story to discount any spiritual empowerment, a solid and rational reason why you will not get healed. The Impostor wants to make your fear-created illusion a material reality, a physical focus, a body thing.

"Hey, look at me, look at the body. You are a body. You must obey the material laws of man and agree with what the doctor said, what the tests show! This was real. A car hit you from behind—this is not a metaphysical game; this was an emergency room event. There were ambulances, medics, police cars, and hospitals. You are a human being, and you must take care of yourself, your body and your health; take some pain pills, fill that prescription for cortisone, get a massage tomorrow, go to physical therapy, and above all, relax and save your knee. And whatever you do, don't use that leg—oh my

God, you will never walk again. What you must do now is find out who is the best knee surgeon in LA, in the world. You may need surgery to walk again. Go home, go to bed, rest... Ice that knee and go lie down."

Sound familiar? The voice of doubt. We have all been there, with ourselves and with our parents, children, and friends.

Same Old Story

I have heard this story so many times in my healing ministry that I can feel the presence of deception, as it speaks. My heart breaks at the unnecessary suffering of my precious clients. Their grief is always resolved by divine action. Let me not exalt myself above humanity—I am subject to these same thoughts; we all are. The Impostor will present its case. Even our Lord Jesus Christ was tempted, but He did not bow to deception.

Back to Mike's Story

Mike was the fiancé of a woman, Carolyn, who was in one of my deliverance groups in Laguna Beach. I knew him by name only. He had never attended the group but was very supportive of her growth. Carolyn encouraged Mike to call me after the accident.

We spoke and he was enthusiastic about sharing his medical x-rays and doctor's opinions. He was very engrossed in the medical diagnosis. It can be very persuasive. Historically, if we check the success of knee surgery and medications for healing the Impostor does not only have many victories. It has very few good testimonies, but it still manages to make itself

Section III: (Part II) Victorious Tales of Divine Retaliation

an authority. It relies solely on the lack of information and the lack of spiritual options for humanity on Earth today.

Mike's consciousness was deep in deception, deep in material, and mental mesmerization. I did not have a plan. I knew what had to happen, but I didn't know how to get him there. He was an athlete, once a very prominent kick boxer, a body-focused individual. It was a blow to him to not to be able to jog, surf, hike, or play volleyball. He was discouraged and depressed.

I invited Mike over for prayer. I needed a show of power from above. I needed some divine intervention to convince him God was in it, one that would encourage him enough to be able to consider and prepare for a retaliation.

Every situation is different, and this is why it is so important to let the spirit lead. Since I had never met Mike in person, I did not know what to expect. He accepted my invitation for prayer, and we made a 7 P.M. appointment.

Mike came over in terrible pain. He was wearing all the prescribed medical gear. He had the neck brace, knee brace, and the smell of lingering Tiger Balm permeated my living room.

I was led immediately to get into prayer. Sometimes talking about the problem can quench the anointing and plan of God. The Impostor is always trying to control the atmosphere with its fear and doubt-filled words and interpretations.

I invited Mike to sit down on a chair in my living room, one that I could walk around from and be able to pray freely without any furniture restrictions. As soon as he sat down, the anointing of God fell upon him. I love when this happens. It is unpredictable, but it meant one thing: there was a predestined healing for Mike. This is my sign that it is done in the spirit, and God was in it in this moment.

The Christos Is Here Now

This is a healer's greatest joy. We were about to go up in the power of the spirit of the living God manifesting His presence. The Christos was being released in healing power. Miracle healing is the grace of God. In deliverance, it is often the carrot of God to bring faith for what God really wants: for you to grow, to step out, and to take territory away from the Impostor, to take what has been taking you, to lay an idol down.

Mike was still wearing all of his medical apparatuses: his neck brace, back support, and knee brace. I began to pray. I was led to pray around Mike's neck first. When I prayed against the spirit of compromise, I felt a deep despair, and as I began to cast it out, I felt Mike's heart open and his breathing become less constricted. I asked him if I could remove the neck brace for the purpose of prayer, and he agreed: a free neck. I then cast out the fear of compromise and the fear of a mind control idol, and at that point, I felt his neck become more relaxed. Mike began to cry, and I knew that Mike's neck had been healed and something else on a deeper level had occurred. I pulled up a chair, and after the crying had subsided, we began to have a serious conversation. Now, Mike was sharing his heart.

Section III: (Part II) Victorious Tales of Divine Retaliation

Mike's Vision

God had given him a vision. Mike had felt the spirit of mind control flee from his neck, as I prayed. Then his mind ceased its constant chatter, and for the moment he had become thoughtless. He described it as a feeling of being stopped in time, a mind suspended.

He then saw himself kickboxing. He was so happy, so alive. Then he was shown all the events he had been invited to, but did not attend, having procrastinated, having given up his kickboxing dreams. Mike saw the instances where he had allowed the rational mind, the Impostor, to undermine the desire of his heart to continue in his professional kickboxing pursuits. He was then seduced into following a career that was not truly in his heart.

Mike said he felt a deep despair about it, but he had not been aware that he was repressing that emotion. Now that he was injured, he believed he would never be able to kick-box again. His heart was deeply saddened that his dream and desire, all his years of preparation and hours of training, could be nullified in a moment by a car accident.

Mike was very grateful for the healing of his neck, but his knee was still very swollen, black, and sore. It had taken the big hit. As he was hit from behind, the knee had been smashed into the dashboard. His doctor had instructed him not to do anymore kickboxing, ever again, and, of course, to stay off the knee as much as he could, unless absolutely necessary—only minor walking. No gym, and no sports.

Your Holy Identity

I prayed again, round two, and with this new information, I was able to go a little deeper. Mike was more receptive. He was now in a surrendered state of mind. Some of the knee swelling and pain was alleviated with this next round of prayer. Mike's neck was free. He was still in a spiritually altered state, and now his spirit was available, and he wanted more of what he was experiencing. This was the first time in Mike's life that he had connected to God with a personal experience. He was ready for more of God, even if he had to do a retaliation to get it. The beauty and the carrot of the Lord can be very persuasive. I prayed again, and this time I asked the Lord to provide another vision for Mike, one that would bring a revelation that would lead to the healing of his knee.

Mike received another kickboxing vision. This time, he was in a kickboxing battle, violently kicking an opponent. It was a spiritual battle. The opposition was dressed in black and kept tenaciously pushing him back. Mike felt sure in his vision that he was losing the battle, and the darkness was huge, like a big dark cloud. It was ubiquitous. He felt powerless next to it. Then he heard the Holy Spirit speak: *"Take your eyes off your opponent; focus totally on me. Give me your mind. Don't take your eyes off me. Keep moving forward into the battle. Just stand strong; do not be moved. Do not be moved in your mind or body."* When Mike did this, he saw a streak of light. It was as if a bolt of lightning had attacked the Impostor. Light had attacked the darkness and had brought all its efforts down. Then the darkness vanished, and so did the cloud of the Impostor.

Mike actually slept for about five minutes while this was going on. When he awakened, his knee was a lot better. The pain had less intensity, and a lot of the swelling was down. It was no longer black, but it was not completely healed. We both saw it as a sign to move ahead and do the actual battle.

Mike's Retaliation

That is exactly what happened: Mike went to his kickboxing gym and this time there was no evil opposition. There was only him, a very battered knee, and the Lord.

He took the big boxing bag and kicked it violently, focusing on the Lord until he knew it was done. It took about forty-five minutes to bring the Impostor under subjugation, until he was sitting high in the spirit in heavenly places in Christ, until the spirit of fear that had created the inflammation on his knee had been worn down, until his knee was perfect, no swelling or bruising at all. In forty-five short but meaningful minutes, the knee was better than new — a renewed kneecap and mind, both having been strengthened by the Holy Ghost.

There was much threatening by the Impostor, much increased swelling during the battle and magnified pain that Mike had to endure. There was much to be conquered. God had met him every step of the way, empowered him more then he had ever hoped for! Mike had the privilege of encountering who he was in Christ!

This is the perk of retaliation. Once you choose to take the land, conquer medical diagnosis and fear, you have favor—

"favor" to be led, favor to hear the voice of God's instruction in the battle, and much added strength and spiritual authority that is needed for the confrontation of evil. This only comes in the battle itself. You can go into a battle with nothing, feel as if you are dying, and come out empowered in victory. It is not about you. If it was, you would not need to go into the battle. You would not need faith, and you certainly would not be retaliating. This is to the glory of God, the grace and power of God undefiled by dogma.

I have some of these word-for-word verbal battles in my personal testimony book, *Enforcing Grace*. In Mike's case, the supernatural and unforeseen perk was that he had not only taken his knee back, which is in and of itself an amazing miracle of faith, but he also had a revelation on how important it is to be true to himself, and has resumed his kickboxing career: the deep desire of his heart. He is now a much happier person.

Chapter 42
Authentic Surrender

When God first came into my life, in a more conscious way, in a way of revelation, he shared my purpose with me. It was exactly this: *"Your purpose in this life, my daughter, is to be in impeccable emotional and spiritual integrity simultaneously."*

I had no idea what that revelation meant. Not a clue! It took me a while to even comprehend it, and my interpretation of it changes as I grow. I have not yet accomplished this task. At first, I thought it would be easy, I wasted much time in the old creature's efforts of trying to correct generationally inherited flaws to fix who I am not.

It is clear to me now that I cannot willfully accomplish my destiny.

I can only go into the refining fire of Christ and allow myself to be sanctified from who I am not. The spirit is always in impeccable integrity.

Integrity is a fruit of the sprit. The same holds true for whatever you are trying to accomplish. When we step into Divine Retaliation, we have given it completely over to God. Then even our jewelry, our adornments, will come under the subjugation of Christ. We will be elevated by the divine short cut of violent faith.

Everything else is just a preparation for that sacred moment of absolute trust and the radical reliance of surrender. I could go on forever writing about divine retaliations. And I will!

As I write this, I am scheduled to stand with a client today to retrieve some relinquished territory. I am led to stop writing about retaliations for this book, If I do not, this book will never be finished!

Take What Is Taking You

If you are trying to figure out where your step of faith is, take what is taking you. If you are trying to figure out where your promotion is, how you can get more power, more love, or more of God, take what is stopping you from moving ahead. If you want more health, more vitality, greater energy, a strong limber body, take what is taking you. If you have a rash, a cold, a weight problem, take what is taking you. If you have cancer, take what is taking you, what has taken you, what has pushed you back, where your heart has been shut down, and your dreams denied, take your essence back.

If I Say Take What Is Taking You…

If I say take what is taking you, or lay the idol down, I am saying the same thing. A loving Creator is on your side, on the side of spiritual reality. God is a spirit. If you want to experience your essence, have favor, change circumstances in your life; if you want to manifest property, love, joy, and radical aliveness, take what is taking you.

Section III: (Part II) Victorious Tales of Divine Retaliation

It may be a small start, a humble beginning: a pair of shoes you cannot wear, a necklace that makes you itchy, medicine that does not help you anyway, a friend that needs to hear your heart, a "no" you need to enforce, with others or in your own mind.

Take back the territory from wherever the Impostor has been seducing you to bow. Take back your expression and where you are giving up your power, where the Impostor would like to have your heart compromised. Take what is holding you back, keeping you stuck, what you are procrastinating: and arrest the fear and doubt you have been listening to by taking a step of faith.

If you want to have mental clarity and sustainable energy, take a little something every day. Keep the attitude of being a daily warrior in your awareness. I have made Divine Retaliation my spiritual practice. The more you take back, the more your energy will be restored, the more your Christos will arise, and the more you will have clarity to see the next "take." I assure you that you will not run out of land. Your territory will start to emerge organically. Retaliation faith is how God keeps us in Him, abiding in the spirit. Divine Retaliation is how we stay in our identity. You cannot live in Christ or have favor without violent faith. You will be continuously backed up by doubt and fear. Fear will not bow to your mortal faith—it does not have to.

"Christos-Sanity" is about walking by faith, walking in a demonstration of our divine rights, aggressively moving ahead, knowing who we are in our Holy Identity, without religion, guilt, and dogma. This is Righteousness Consciousness, The

Perfect Law of Liberty, without the idols of mind control. It is inclusive of miracle healing, emotional transformation, divine love, and spiritual purpose. You cannot do it better, grow faster, go higher, or help yourself to de-victimize the generational impostor's strongholds. Righteousness Consciousness provides an opportunity for dominion on Earth, now.

> *"Seek ye first the Kingdom of God and His*
> *righteousness and all else will be added unto you."*
> —Matt. 6:33

About the Author

Reverend Juliana Taylor, Ph.D., is both a clinical psychologist and a Marriage and Family therapy counselor. She was born in New York City and is a graduate of Pepperdine and Brunel Universities.

She lived and worked in Los Angeles for many years as a psychologist, she was trained in Transactional analysis, Gestalt therapy, and behavior therapy, and having completed a two-year internship in Emotional Release Therapy work, with Chuck and Erica Kelly, at the Radix Institute in Ojai, California.

Dr. Taylor completed advanced training programs and workshops with Claude Steiner and Denton Roberts, at All Peoples Church, in downtown Los Angeles. She also completed a two-year internship, at Resthaven Psychiatric Hospital, in Los Angeles, where she received her work training hours for her Marriage and Family Therapy counseling license. It was there that she was trained and received a certificate in drug, alcohol and addiction counseling.

Rev. Juliana was a pioneer in the early years of the stress reduction movement, incorporating biofeedback and meditation into her practice, and established Stress Centers in both Los Angeles and New York City.

After years of commitment to her work and her clients, she became deathly ill. Juliana was discouraged and despondent to find that all of her years of introspection, stress reduction work, and personal therapy did little to help her in a personal health crisis.

She was diagnosed with lupus, environmental illness, Epstein Barr Virus, chronic fatigue syndrome, and food allergies. She found herself living in utter isolation in the hills of Santa Barbara. She was dying!

After years of having diverse medical interventions and many immune system clinics, she was told that her immune system had collapsed, and her organs were malfunctioning to such an advanced degree that she would never recover. At that point, she had gotten down to sixty pounds, and being told that there was nothing more they could do for her, she was sent home to die.

It was at that point of desperation that she had her personal encounter with Christ. It was then that, piece by piece, revelation to revelation, she was healed and restored. She was restored by discovering her true identity, who she truly was, a spiritual being in Righteousness Consciousness in Christ.

Juliana was led to confront her illnesses by violent faith, by the faith of the spirit!

After her personal healing demonstrations, she was called to the ministry of healing and deliverance.

She was discipled at and became a Co-Pastor of "World for Christ" ministries in Newbury Park, Ca.

About the Author

She is a spiritual activist and the founder of Enforcing Grace Ministries. She and her team are involved with imparting the knowledge and power of our divine rights on Earth, for all people.

Her work reflects her opposition to the deceptions of manmade religion and Sin Consciousness in the church and everywhere else on Earth. She is purposed to enlarge our understanding of Righteousness Consciousness and thereby to undermine and annihilate the intent of Sin Consciousness and its works of despair, illness, fear, and condemnation in the world today.

To contact this ministry:
www.revjulianataylorphd.com
www.enforcinggrace.com
revjulianantaylor@gmail.com
YouTube: revjulianataylorph.d
Facebook: revjulianataylorphd.
"Enforcing Grace" @ Amazon.com

www.ingramcontent.com/pod-product-compliance
Lightning Source LLC
Chambersburg PA
CBHW060455090426
42735CB00011B/1994